WE THE CORRUPT PEOPLE

D. RENZI

Trafford PUBLISHING®   www.trafford.com

North America & international
toll-free: 1 888 232 4444 (USA & Canada)
phone: 250 383 6864 ♦ fax: 812 355 4082 ♦ email: info@trafford.com

Acknowledgement

Much thanks to Brenda Erhardt and Trudy Pascoe for their valuable help, and wonderful patience with me in my literary endeavor.

All proceeds from this book will be donatied to children with disabilities, and other needy kids.

The author is the writer of three other books, and wishes to remain anonymous.

Preface

I + I = 2

Perhaps a good beginning would be what I have copied from my Merriam-Webster Dictionary, 1998 Edition.

I looked up the word "Corrupt", and "Corruption". The definition of both words are as follows – To make evil, to deprave, especially bribery, to rot, spoiled. Also under the word "Corruption" is, morally degenerate, improper conduct, esp. officials.

I also looked up the meanings of the word "Bribe". And the definition of the word "Bribe" is, something stolen, something as money or a favor, given or promised to a person to influence conduct. To influence by offering a "bribe" is the Second definition.

Then I looked up the word "Lobby". Most people are familiar with lobbyist, and lobbying the Congress or other influential public officials, from the lowest form of Government up to higher public officials in the higher branches of Government.

And the definition of "lobbying" is, "to attempt to influence public officials, especially legislators". And I looked up the words or phrase commonly used in Washington, quotes commonly used by writers of Newspaper or magazine articles, probably, an expression not understood by the ordinary citizen. The expression is "Quid Pro Quo", defined in the dictionary as "something for something", something given, or received, for something else.

Now with those definitions in mind, and regarding my following experiences, you may put them in a file, according to how grave the incidents may be, possibly a rating system from 1 to 10, as to the gravity of these incidents – I leave it to the reader.

Perhaps the following song we sang as youngsters in school is in order, with my revised lyrics to "My Country Tis of Thee".

My Country tears for thee
Corrupt land of depravity
For Thee I weep
Land where our Fathers strived
But evilness also rived
O'er every bit of Country side
Let the death knell ring.

AFFIRMATION OF FACTS

In writing of my experiences with corrupt practices of all kinds, all are factual happenings. Though I may not remember dates and times, nevertheless, all are accurate and the truth.

I do know the names, but in many cases have changed them. I have done this for 2 reasons. At this late date, 50 years or more, and some less, I do not want to open a can of worms to harm families of those who perpetrated the event mentioned. I also do not wish my doors to get smashed in by those who would seek to do me harm. I have used a non-de-plume as author.

However the names are available and are put in a safe place in the event of proof of my writings and pronouncement of corruption is necessary.

I would hope the reader will separate the happenings of events from my opinions, which are formed because of my experiences with the stated occurrences in the following pages.

In The Beginning

As I begin this treatise on my experiences with corruption, I perhaps should start with my earliest recollection, and proceed in a chronological order as I grew older, and the experiences that took place at varying stages of my life, continuing to this day – thus enabling me to add 1+1 to form opinions of current events taking place in all branches of local, state and federal government, including big business.

My earliest recollection concerning the content of this book, took place when I was 3-4 years old. On leaving my house to play with other kids, I saw them clustered in front of the house across the street, so I joined them. They were excited and scared at the same time, exclaiming about a "Black Hand" painted on the front entryway to the house. The black hand was the "logo" of the Sicilian Mafia, and usually meant someone in that house had transgressed in some way or another, and unless the transgressor refrained from whatever he was doing to irritate the mafia – it was a dire warning – do what we say – or else!

My family knew and were friends with that family. We kids played with their kids, shared homes and meals with each other. We knew them for years, as just nice people. They ran a popular Italian bakery which we frequented more times than I can count – so this sign on the front of the house was a very big surprise to all in the area. But of course we knew nothing of the private lives of these people, and being kids – what did we know anyway? And if the adults in the area knew anything, they sure weren't talking!

So let me jump ahead in this one instance, to a time somewhere when I was attempting to play jazz harmonica, meeting jazz musicians and attending concerts where these musicians played, sometimes sitting in and playing with them. By this time I was about 60 years old. I went to a club in Hollywood, and met one of the foremost trumpet – cornet players of all time, Bobby Hackett. I had met him years prior, through my brother, who was also a jazz afficianado, and a neighbor of Hackett.

We sat together all night, swapping stories, mostly of music and the people back home. During our reminiscences, the conversation turned to the bad experiences musicians had with people in some clubs with the owners – many who were mafia figures. Bobby Hackett said, "I never have to worry about getting paid, I don't worry about any trouble at all, I just show them this". Bobby reached into his watch pocket, pulled out the watch fob, and showed me the medallion on the end of the strap. It was an enameled fob with the replication of the Black Hand, with the code or motto of that society imprinted above each finger. Bobby said, "I never have a bit of a hassle when they see this".

Like me, Bobby Hackett grew up in an area of the country that is known as one of the mafia controlled organizational areas, where a Boss runs all the gambling, and whatever else the mafia is involved in. And like me, probably went to school or played sports when young, with the people involved in mafia activities. Being a well known musician, featured for years on recordings, and also heading many musical bands and small groups in the big band era, and afterwards – he most likely was well liked by the mafia figures – and though not Mafioso himself, was given the Black Hand medallion as a token of a neighbor who was admired for making it big in the music world, and a nice guy they knew from the old days when they were kids and neighbors, something akin to the above happened to me, which I will relate further on.

Between my above early age, and most likely before, my Dad worked on the "Banana boats". They ran to South America, and usually on his return, brought a big box of bananas home, and would place them in back of the kitchen stove to ripen. He brought them for we 6 kids. In between boat trips, he also made trips to another state to pick up bootleg booze. The car he drove had concealed tanks to transport the alcoholic beverages. It was his side job. One of the people who went with him was Joseph Kennedy, father of President John Kennedy. Old man Kennedy and my Dad were long time old friends, played baseball and football together. They played on one of the oldest pro-football clubs in the country, being champions in their league in 1906 – I have a photo of that championship team portraying among the teammates, Joe Kennedy. My Dad says Joe Kennedy missed many practices and some games, for he was always studying various books at home, a real book worm.

Sometime between 7 and 9 years old I chummed around with 2 brothers, a year or two older than I, neighbors of ours. One Saturday when school was closed, we went to the schoolyard to play. After a while I noticed a line of kids, 15-20 at the entrance to a stairwell outside the school, that led down into the school basement. Out of curiosity, I went over to see what was going on, as the school was closed. At the bottom of the stairs was one of the brothers giving oral sex to any kid – hence the long line. I watched as the older brother laughed, and said, "He does that to me all the time". I walked away, sick to my stomach – and vomited. That was my first experience to witnessing moral degeneracy. The family moved away shortly thereafter!

At the same time as above, I remember the duo called Sacco and Vanzetti. The area of the city we lived in was about split between Irish immigrant and Italian families. So there was much controversy regarding the guilt or innocence of these men, who were convicted of being bomb-throwing anarchists. Being young and unknowing of the events concerning adults, I didn't understand a thing about these men, only what one heard in news broadcasts or headlines, and didn't concern kids. But I do remember the execution night, as many lights went out all over the city when they pulled the switches to execute these two men. I remember there were protests everywhere. Witnessing all the turmoil, the scary thought in this little kids head was, "Boy I hope I never have to go to prison!" Ironically, at that time there was a popular song we sang, and knew all the lyrics, "The Prisoners Song"!!

I began to become more interested in sports, and it wasn't very long before I could understand, even sports hero's were morally corrupt. I remember being disappointed in heavyweight boxing champion Jack Sharkey who, it was claimed, won the championship by a supposed foul blow he took below the belt. Then all the fixed wrestling matches, so that wrestling today has degenerated into a clown's demonstration of acrobatic tricks. Over the years I've watched many fights that were nothing more than set-ups so the gamblers in control can make money while a real good boxer has to "take a dive" for the gamblers. Then the Black Sox scandal, and on and on in "sports" of all kinds, until today with all the accusations of our paper heroes taking all kinds of drugs to enhance their performance. No more Ted Williams, Joe DiMaggio, Babe Ruth, Lou Gehrigs! Only phonies.

Along with the above sports comments, I would add one more incident. I jump ahead a few years. About the 8th grade, I and 2 other of my classmates were given tickets to the baseball writers dinner, an annual affair in the big city. Why? To this day I don't know. And also don't know why the teacher, who was responsible for we three getting these tickets, kept the three of us after school for a whole year, just to help him put on his topcoat! We weren't unruly, hadn't been disruptive, nothing! But nevertheless we were stuck after school every day – and for some strange reason, got tickets for the dinner – also accompanied by the Vice-Principal of the school! Don't ask me why – But naturally, being at the dinner we wanted to meet some of the Major League ballplayers, most of whom we did. But the down side was, in looking for ballplayers to get their autographs, we followed two for most of the night, but they evaded us all night, until we finally caught them coming off the hotel elevator. We pleaded with them for autographs. One Al Simmons who was a home run hitter, and was chasing Babe Ruth's record, and a hero of his time, started cursing us in no uncertain terms, using the most foul language, totally unexpected, and a very dismaying shock to we kids. Our hero saying that rotten stuff to us? What a come down! Needless to say – though he signed his name, I didn't want it! The other player, "Goose" Goslin, was friendly and smiling and talked with us. But again, my faith in people sunk another notch. Who needs a half drunk ballplayer swearing at kids?

Before reading the next section dealing with corruption, let me say – There are many, many good people in this country and I have been blessed with many great friends – they keep me sane, for though they are out there everywhere, we are still inundated with the corruption – and never forget – corruption's master is money!

My Family bought a house on the other side of the river in 1930. A new, hopefully better town, with parks, lots of trees, grass lawns, prettier homes, and fewer tenements, and outwardly, a much better environment, though I would be subject to the old environment in many ways.

Our next-door neighbors were nice people, on one side a Police Lieutenant, whose son was a lawyer, and the daughter a schoolteacher. I was given much by the family, a flexible flyer sled, Chicago roller skates, sports equipment and games shared with my now 7 siblings.

The other side neighbors were a fine Jewish family, very caring people, and owners of a Salvage yard. The wife gave me many jobs to do just so I could give the money to my Mom, as it was the Great Depression starting, unknown at that date. I often wonder if those depression days were the start of corruption – as I firmly believe corruption starts with the little guy – the guy who has nothing, and so has to go to the man above him to get something desperately needing, in order to pay the rent, get a job, or rein in someone attempting to do him harm, or any number of things out of reach. It always involves money, or the repaying of a favor. For friends don't ask anything of you – just reciprocated friendship.

Along with the good neighbors, came realization that there were others not so nice. My teenage years were a great learning period.

However honest and caring of the Police Lieutenant and his family, there was another cop, 4 houses down the street, who had 5 or 6 kids, but was an alcoholic, which resulted in much family troubles, and eventually his being fired after many years of service, because he would report to duty under the influence of the booze.

In those days, Cops walked their beats, no patrol cars, and all us kids knew all the Cops – and they knew everyone of us. They knew any body who had minor scuffles, the kids who were smart asses, the good kids – and they were always respectful and basically friendly, talking to us all the time – umpire games for us for an inning or two – and we respected them, along with the fear of them reporting anything of a doubtful nature to our parents. Some of the kids we hung out with had Dads who were cops. So one had better behave, and the greater part of us did. However, there were the other kind.

There was another Cop with the same name as a Mounted Policeman on a popular radio program. He was an excellent detective also, and so he was sent to the FBI academy in Washington D.C. to study with them for 6 months. He returned and made an excellent detective, with a wonderful reputation for solving all sorts of crimes.

While working in a restaurant one day, I saw the bookies who worked in the downtown area, collecting betting money for the "number pool", horse and dog bets, treasury numbers, baseball, football and all types of illegal betting, come running into the restaurant, yipping and hollering, giving each other "high fives", and saying, "we got him!!" over and over. Being puzzled about the commotion, I asked one of the bookies what all the excitement was about. He replied over and over, "We got him, we got him"!

Still not knowing, I asked, "Got who – what are you talking about?" "Ace! – Ace!" (Not his real name) "We got him – took us ten years, but we got him!!" Then I got it! They had "bought" the famous dedicated detective for money – now they wouldn't have to be arrested or investigated for any illegal bookmaking in the city. So much for "honest Cops!!"

There were many times I'd be in a café with some friends, just relaxing, talking about our war service, family, etc. Then the phone would ring, and the bartender would holler "Everyone out, there's going to be a raid by the State Cops!" The reason – betting was illegal in any form, except at horse or dog racing tracks. But every barroom, even restaurants, had racing forms, newspapers, green sheets, and Armstrong racing forms. All these had information of all kinds, from Horse or Dogs names, owners, jockeys, past performances, win – losses, so that one could read these and make a bet with the bookie – and every place had a bookie!

You didn't have to go to the racetrack, and you could bet horses at any track in the country – from Suffolk Downs in Mass., or Rockingham in N.H., to west coast and everywhere in between. You could bet 50 cents on win-place-show, or any place you wanted. At the track you would pay $2.00 per bet – In the bars you could play 50 cents – as win - $2.00 place - $2.00 show $2.00 at the track – in the bars win 50 cents - place 50 cents – show 50 cents – only you didn't get track odds – bookies paid less – but if you were lucky, you could make money and save track entrance fees. It was a good thing for the poor man who enjoyed betting on horses or dogs.

So when the bartender hollered "everyone out!" – all the racing forms disappeared with the customers, and when the State Cops got there on their "surprise raid"- Surprise!, there was no one but the bartender!

Just another bit of corruption by someone in the State police department tipping off the bookies about a coming "raid!!"

In the numbers game, you could bet from 1 cent on up on any 3 or 4 numbers that were listed in the evening papers, after the tracks closed. 5 cents would win $30.00 dollars. I had a new truck on another job I had, with new license plates with 4 numbers. I played the 4 numbers and won for the only time in my life - $250.00 for my 25-cent bet! Best of all – it was the week before Christmas!! That really made my holiday!! Gifts for everybody!

We friends went to cafes that had a piano player on the weekends, as we all liked to get up at the mike and sing. It was pretty common to see the cop on the beat come in to the café, not looking left or right, head for the kitchen – a couple of minutes later the waitress would bring a double shot or two into the kitchen and ten minutes later the Cop would leave just as he had come in – nose a little redder than before – especially in the winter!

There was also a cop we knew, as we played ball together when we were kids. He was on the force for a number of years, but never made a single arrest. He always walked the other way, even when observing a burglary in progress – especially if he knew them or were his friends – he was fired!

One of my brother's friends was also on our local police force. His uncle bought pure alcohol, which he would cut with water, add a flavor to it, and sell it to friends and neighbors. That was stronger than anything you could buy in a store – it could also kill you! But many did that, and it was a common practice among Italians. I've had it many times – it has the kick of the mule!!

I would like to interject here, how, in my mind, corruption starts. It starts with the little guy – the powerless person, who has no money, no connections to people who can help him when in need, and however desperate the need, must turn to those that can help – the person above him that does have the connections that will help him with his problem, however great or small. Remember the famous quote, "it isn't what you know, it's who you know". So it's the little guy who corrupts the big guy – and that usually involves money, or a favor for a favor – Quid Pro Quo – something for something. So in practice, the big powerful moneymen in Big Business, become the little guy who needs the big guy politicians to get a bill passed so they can profit – hence the Quid Pro Quo – something for something.

A good example of the above – which many people probably paid no attention to, comes from the first movie of the "Godfather", with Marlon Brando. In the beginning minutes of the movie, an old man goes to visit the Godfather because some macho young guy is messing with his daughter, and he is fearful for her safety. The Godfather tells the old man not to worry; he'll take care of everything. The old man is very effusive in his thanks, and starts to leave the office. Just before he leaves the room, the door half open, the Godfather says, "Maybe someday you can do me a favor". There is the sealed contract – the above something for something!

To illustrate the above, let me tell you of a couple of instances where I also am guilty, as many of us are, of engaging in corruption or doing something unlawful, though in many instances we are not caught. I learned to drive when I was fourteen years old – I learned by driving a truck, double clutching while shifting gears, down shifting to slow the truck, etc. I drove for 15 years, off and on, borrowing cars from friends, when we were kids, to go to a distant beach, or some other occasion, like going to see a Big Band, or Dance.

Transportation, buses, trolleys, the subway trains were our main method of commuting, and the service was good, and being broke during the Depression days, very few could afford an automobile, it was a luxury afforded only by those business people who worked every day or those with a steady job. Even in my WWII days I never had a license to drive until I got overseas, and even then I never took a test – just told them I could drive, and was issued a license.

Finally at age 29, I got a job as a mechanic with my Brother in Law and was told I would have to drive a tow truck. He made an appointment with the Motor Vehicle Department – I went there, asked for a certain person, no test at all, I got my license – Just like that! You will understand the connection later, as you read on.

I would like to digress here for a bit, a very important bit, as I look at my Country and what it has become. Up until I entered the C.C.C. after graduating high school, as no jobs were available – most of all kids I knew, almost never got out at night. I was allowed Friday night out, and only to go to the Y.M.C.A. till 9 PM, and if I got home 1 minute late, the door was locked and my Dad usually answered when I rang the doorbell. I always got a backhander, and if I ever lied about my lateness, I got more than a few backhanders. I learned from an early age – Always tell the truth – you better believe it's a lesson well learned! My point in this being, we kids had the same type of no-nonsense parents, for as my Dad said many times, "I pulled that trick before you were born"! So I didn't smoke until I was 16 – the permissible date back them – none of us drank – none had girl friends or messed around in any way until around the age of 18. I only knew one other person, not our friend, who occasionally used marijuana, and knew only one hooker in our town!

12

Sure there were those who you knew would eventually do something in the way of sex – but it would be in the hope of their getting married! In those days marriage was unaffordable, so we never messed with the girls. I don't even remember any out of wedlock babies!

I remember one embarrassing item – I bought a condom, being ashamed when doing so, as they were behind the counter, and you had to ask the druggist for them in those days. I bought it "just in case"! One day my Mom was emptying my suit pockets as she was taking my suit to the cleaners, she found the condom, which by this time was 2-3 years old. She told my Dad, and he asked me about it. I told him I'd been carrying it for a couple of years "just in case" and he never said a word. We just looked at the frayed pack, which no doubt would have been very ineffectual, even though I needed it "just in case"! To sum up – sure we kicked up our heels on occasion, but we were a fairly straight bunch of kids. For others and myself we always had to answer to our parents. I only feared and respected 2 people in my life – one was God – the other was my Dad – and he was there all the time, in the flesh! And boy! Could he hit!

I would like to relate my first encounter with a predatory homosexual person, as that is what homos are, Evil Predators! I can't count the number of times in my life I've been approached by these degenerates. They should dump them on some far away island and let them orgy themselves to death!

I was 13 years old, and hung out at a so-called park with kids of all ages. There were no trees or shrubbery, just a big gravely space, fenced in, with swings, see-saws for younger kids, and where we played all our sports, even to having various sports leagues, playing against other teams in the city who had their own similar playgrounds. Ours was 200 yards from my house.

There was one male and one female adult person, who taught or umpired games, watched over the younger kids and monitored the activities as best they could. They were former athletes put to work by the city, to make jobs for unemployed people during the Depression. There were other adults, who frequented the park, to observe, or help out when needed, and some were parents of kids. One such person had been to the Seminary to become a Priest, but for some unknown reason hadn't made it. He always hung around my group, and because we knew he was trying for the Priesthood, had a lot of childish respect for him, both as a mentor and a friend we looked up to. His brother frequented the park also, as did another buddy of the wannabe Priest, so adult presences was the norm.

One day while waiting for my buddies, he approached me and asked if I were fooling around with girls? I told him no, I had no interest – I had 5 sisters at home, that was enough for me! He kept insisting I must be fooling around with girls, despite my denials, and I wondered, why this questioning about girls? Then he said, I must be fooling around and playing with myself! My 13-year-old mind kept saying "Huh? As this nutty questioning went on, something clicked in my head, I didn't know what it was, but something didn't make sense, as this innocent kid hadn't the slightest clue as to what he was talking about! He said he didn't believe me, and to make sure I wasn't playing with myself, he told me to take a piece of string when I was home, and measure my "thing"! Now it was a great big "HUH"? The alarm bells went off! What the heck is he talking about? String? Measure my "thing"? He told me I would have to keep measuring my "thing" to make sure I wasn't lying to him. How many pieces of string did he want? This is crazy – what in heck is he talking about ran through my mind. Whatever it was, it wasn't right, said my mind.

I thought, if I ever tell my Mom or Dad about this, my Dad would kill him, beat him to a pulp, because something was wrong and I didn't know what, just the wrong feeling I had, and I didn't want my Dad in jail, it was a gut feeling I had in my dumb head! So I never told a soul – only did I tell one of my sisters just 3 years ago, and I am 86!

But he kept asking me for weeks, where is the string, over and over again. I always made up an excuse, we had no string, or I couldn't find the scissors, or whatever. I just had this gut feeling, so kept lying, which was hard, as my Dad pounded it into me – always tell the truth! Finally some weeks later, someone caught him and his buddy having oral sex in an alleyway between two houses, and I was never bothered again! What happened to him? He joined the Navy in WWII, after which he did become a Priest, and passed away in his early 30's. The Man upstairs never forgets – he is the final arbiter!

At age 17, and upon graduation from High School, no jobs being available for this unskilled guy, who probably didn't look more than 12, I joined the C.C.C. (Civilian Conservation Corps.), a Government program to put unemployed young men to work, mostly in forestry, road building, making new, and working in current National Parks. I went to Colorado, helped build a dam (that is still in use today), worked with ranchers, planted trees, worked in a tree nursery, sign shop, and as an officers cook and orderly. We operated exactly as the U.S. Army, except that we did the above work instead of drilling or learning the art of war.

The only item of corruption I recall was that of a Reserve Cavalry officer who was our C.O., and depriving us of the little food we were allotted, by skimping on our meals, with cheap food, and the sameness of skimpy, non-nourishing food. And as we worked long hours, pick and shovel mostly, and hard labor all day, the food was not nearly enough for us. Instead, he was pocketing some of the money, and buying cheap food with the rest. One night we all dumped our food in unison, and the resulting furor led to an investigation, where our C.O. was dumped and another took his place, which was a big improvement.

The only other item was the Legal Brothels in Pueblo, on 2 streets. We frequented them maybe one a month, as we had little money. But we would go in, drop a nickel in the jukebox and dance with the "girls". Some older guys did more. But to stay in business, there had to be a kickback to City officials, or they wouldn't have "legalized" the prostitution!

The only hate crime I witnessed was prior to W.W.II. There was much "Hilterite" speeches and propaganda in newspapers, radio, magazines, and there were those few who got sucked in by this rot.

I was on my way to work, and as I left my house, a fellow was also leaving his house, and was about 100 feet in front of me. When he got to the corner of our street, 2 Irish wise guys I was familiar with, jumped this neighbor who was Jewish. They attacked him from behind. They were real tough guys in their late teens, and big. My Jewish neighbor fought back and proceeded to land some powerful blows on his attackers – so much so that he drove them off, as he proved not to be a helpless Jew, but a tough guy in his own right. The two thugs fled the scene, and it was over before I could get there. I told my neighbor, I knew the guys if he wanted to press charges, but he declined, saying they hadn't hurt him at all – a pretty tough guy!

A Change of Lifestyle —
but no change

Shortly after the above incident, Pearl Harbor was attacked, and so my experience in how good the Navy ate prompted me to enlist in that service, but my Mom wouldn't agree to anything where I was on the high seas, due to the many ships being sunk, right off our own shores. The only papers they would sign were for the Air Corps. I went to school to become an Aircraft Mechanic, though I wanted to fly.

It was a different set of rules and law in the Military. I saw little difference in that law, as I had been in the C.C.C. for a year under Military Officers, so was easily adaptive to the lifestyle, plus my Dad's influence was a good training for me, as the first thing I learned was, "Do as you're told, and ask questions afterwards". That was so true. There were many small instances of unfair orders, or decisions, that I will only mention a few.

After graduating from Aircraft Mechanic's School at Chanute Field, Il., I became a propeller specialist at a factory school where the prop for the P-39 Aircobra fighter was made.

Then the transfer to the B-25 Bomber Group I was to serve in for 3 years, until WWII ended. Being the 3rd prop specialist, and the tech order only calling for two, I went out to the flight line to learn the B-25. We trained at 4 different bases in the Southern U.S., then shipped overseas for a 2 ½ year stint, til wars end.

The following excerpts are occurances of ineptness, moral corruption, and the realization that no matter what the circumstances or change in occupation or lifestyle – the same old, same old, continues unabated. Really a war on two fronts!

Though there were many heroes, wonderful pilots, combat crew members who out shone all the negative aspects of Military life, many of who are dear friends to this day, I merely point out the negatives to show that corruption of one kind or another exists everywhere. The most common all service men suffer is "Rank Pulling", which is simply a man with higher rank that uses his higher rank to benefit himself, unduly harass others, or simply to show he's the boss, whether right or wrong – and most times they are wrong!

Though I'm not complaining now, and didn't then, my confrontation with my Captain is a good case in point, and that wouldn't have happened if I were sober, as I will relate later.

One other point – there were many of us who never saw home in 3-5 years! We spent 4 Christmases in the service, never got a day at home in all that time. All that inequity due to inefficient Officers and flawed policy, where rank counted more that doing the right thing for those of lesser ranks or status.

I don't know anyone entering the Air Force who doesn't want to fly. As a kid I collected all I could about flying, read books and magazines, saw all the WWI movies about flying aces exploits, visited the Main airport in the big city, marveled at all the planes I saw, even climbing in Cockpits, dreaming of flying. Long before it became an international airport, I would sit in these planes and no one stopped you – there were no fences or personnel guarding against this, and those I would meet were very friendly and informative with me, imparting much knowledge to this young teenager. So in these long years growing up and finally being in the Air Corps, my dreams of flying appeared to becoming true.

Little did I know how soon my hopes would be dashed. After being sworn in at the recruiting station… off on a train to Fort Devens, Massachusetts for a myriad of tests, clothing and the first of many lies we would hear for the duration, coupled with the first of many shots in the arm. I can still hear, after fifty eight years, a Lt. Firestone saying, "Men…This general classification test doesn't mean anything…we just want to get an idea of what you know". He also stressed the importance of getting correct answers to a minimum of four math questions. The test was a cinch…except I stunk at math! Concentrating on the math, picking those I knew were right…I ran out of time…so only answered approximately 120 of 150 questions. My score was 108…but as the Lt. said, the test didn't matter…so began the quest for a pair of wings!

From basic training at that first base, within 3 days we were sent to another Basic Training Center, arriving on Christmas morning. We were promised we could go home for Christmas at the first base, but that promise was broken, and here we were, our first lesson of how the Services easily and with no care at all of breaking their word, sent us 1200 miles to a new base instead.

Following our Basic, we were sent to another base to study to be Aircraft Mechanics. Again, my hopes of being a pilot were dashed, as pilot training required a college education. In the beginning a degree, later on as the war progressed those standards were lowered to 1 year of college for all flying officers, was sufficient for pilot training.

Some men including me, came down with "yellow jaundice". Our barracks was quarantined for a week, so we missed seven days of school. We spent the time playing baseball and football, then I and three other wound up in the base hospital for treatment. We had a very enjoyable time flirting with the nurses, who were very caring, did everything to ease our comfort. I think they wised up quickly when we all asked for a back rub and massage.

When released from the hospital, a few of us decided that as we had missed seven of our ten day phase, we would take the other three days off. We had a great time at the service club dancing with the hostesses to the Big Band music on the Juke Box, even worked our way out of the front gate to visit Rantoul, and more girls.

We got "nailed" – and had to report to our Squadron C.O. We went to the orderly room, and individually went in to the C.O.'s office, smartly saluted and stated, "Private Renzi, serial number 12345678, reporting as ordered

Sir". The C.O. queried us as to our reason for "skipping school". When we told him we would only repeat the three days again, so decided to wait til the missed phase was repeated, we were found "guilty" and sentenced to "hard labor" for a week – which consisted of sweeping the streets of our School Squadron, K.P. and other assorted nuisance duties. This was the only infraction on my war record, and a lesson well learned. It reinforced the old Army adage – "Do what you're told – ask questions afterwards"!

While at Chanute, a notice appeared on the orderly room bulletin board… "All those who wish to apply for cadet pilot training, report to chief clerk. Your general classification test score must be 110!" Oh, baby, how I hated Lt. Firestone at Ft. Devens, who said, "your score doesn't mean a thing, we just want an idea of what you know." Someone should have given him a test to see how much he knew!

Probably, one of the most enduring negative memories I have of Chanaute Field is the time my good friend Joe Lemois from Providence, RI, and I went to Peoria, Illinois, on a weekend. We caroused around, chasing 'B'-girls, dancing to swing music, and imbibing too much, so that we wound up at a bar that was a meeting place for our ride back to Chanute on Sunday morning. We were bushed, bleary eyed and broke!

Our barracks Chief, a big 6'2", 280 lb. behemoth, told us we looked terrible. When we told him why, he said he would let us use an apartment he had, for a couple of hours sleep, then we could get a ride back to the base. As he was our boss, and brooked no nonsense, always the typical stern Sergeant, barking orders ... we figured we had better do what he said ... so we ambled down to his apartment.

I was really tired from the carousing around all week-end, so wasted no time in undressing down to my skivvies and getting into bed, while Joe went into the other bedroom. I had slept in the same bed with my brothers, cousins, and other GIs when we couldn't afford more than one room...so it didn't bother me when the Sarge said he also should grab a few hours sleep, and lay down in my bed.

I had just about dozed off, when his arm lay across my body, so I pushed it off, only to have it return again, firmer this time...and I said, "Hey, move over, you're taking up too much room", and started to doze again. Then came a leg, and I pushed that away, and moved toward the edge of the bed. More arms and legs followed and I began to wonder. I lit a cigarette, hoping he'd fall asleep while I smoked. But he lit one also, and I began to worry. I smoked till the cigarette was ½ inch long, and my fingers began to burn. By this time I figured I was in trouble! Laying down again, the arms and legs started their work again, and I was up against the bedroom wall. This guy was 7 inches taller and over 100 pounds heavier than me...I was scared out of my mind...with all sorts of bad things happening to me...I panicked...I saw vivid red...I was ready to kill! I broke free somehow...jumped up and standing in my shorts in the middle of the bed, I snarled, "you lay a hand on me and I'll beat the living hell out of you". I didn't know how this 150 lb. weakling was going to do it...but at that moment I'd have taken on King Kong! I was raging mad...and all of a sudden he started to cry! He went to Joe's room...I jumped off the bed…grabbed my clothes and headed for the door. Just then Joe walked out of his room saying, "Did you have to send him in to me?" Needless to say, I never got KP again, or any detail…but I was told the Sergeant had been molesting some other young recruit.

Ed Lefebvere from Lowell, MA., who was a few years older than Joe and I, had also accompanied us to Peoria. Not long after arriving there, we lost Ed. We looked everywhere for him to no avail. Upon returning to Chanute Field, we learned of Ed's disappearance.

Ed had stopped into a bar to have one drink. He finished the drink, went outside and passed out on the sidewalk. He awoke in the hospital in Peoria – the bartender had slipped him a "Mickey" – but Ed had managed to get outside of the bar before it hit him, preventing him from being "rolled" for his money. What most infuriated Ed, was the Red Cross notifying his family of the incident and billing them for a weeks hospital stay. Ed vowed he'd never donate to the Red Cross again!

Definition of Rank Pulling – Rank Pulling for a simple definition, is someone of a higher rank, or position, simply to use his rank for the self-service of himself, whether right or wrong – most times wrong! As being in a long line in a supermarket, or theater, and someone steps in front of all waiting their turn – just like Illegal Immigration!

Early December, and a move to a new base where the many cross-country trips were made to perfect navigational skills. Many guys got to visit home, as one living in an area the plane was scheduled to go, were usually picked for the flight. I was aced out of the Boston trip by a rank-pulling 2nd Lt. who didn't live within a hundred miles of the airport. I could have hit my house with a rock! There was also the problem of furloughs… many men had earned 30 day furloughs, but, as we were working on the line all day, we never knew about them till we got to the squadron area at night, and they were all gone. This happened a number of times, and was very discouraging, morale took a big hit. This writer complained and it followed him to the end of the war. Many others and I served anywhere from 3-6 years and never got to see family in all that time. After the latest furlough fiasco, we knew in our gut it wouldn't be very long before going overseas.

Our Squadron CO was nicknamed 'Black Mack'. To save embarrassment to him, his moniker shall suffice for this event, as it was one of the darkest periods of our Squadron History. 'Black Mack' was a very strict taskmaster, who tolerated no mistakes, very uncompromising in his stern efforts in running our squadron. He was our commanding officer's favorite pilot, building up his reputation and respect in the ranks for him, by his relentless pursuit of perfection from all men.

There are many versions of this period, but essentially everything boils down to the fact 'Black Mack' didn't want to go overseas. He didn't want to leave his wife whom he loved very much. At one point over water, it is reported he attempted to lead the squadron into the water, in what some call a suicide dive of his B-25. The co-pilot forcefully took over the controls preventing a disaster to the Group who were following him.

On arrival overseas, as was operational procedure, planes taxied out for mission take off, checked out all instruments and engines on run-up. This was always done on our pre-flight procedure, and any malfunction would immediately negate that plane being on a mission. So the run-up before take off was a double check for safety's sake. On every run-up 'Black Mack' would find something wrong with his engines and abort the mission. The onus was on his mechanic, but every time the engines were rechecked, nothing was found to be malfunctioning. His continual aborts made the mechanics look bad. Adding to this was bad feelings developing among the pilots that our CO was a coward. Morale dropped throughout the squadron…pilots looked askance at each other, the ground crews, and mistrust set in, especially regarding the merit of the mechanics. Finally 'Black Mack' was relieved of command, sent back to the States, leaving a much demoralized squadron in his propwash. It took a long while before normalcy returned and confidence was instilled in aircrews as to the mechanic's expertise, and their own trust in others of the combat crews.

As with many of our original pilots at Columbia, S.C., in our early days of training, Bob my pilot had much flying experience prior to Pearl Harbor Day.

Early in May '43 when I became a crew chief, Bob was assigned to my plane as First Pilot. We both had much training together, along with approximately 30 missions under his belt, and I as the assistant crew chief on "Booger", our first plane.

Bob flew our new plane until he finished his 50 missions and went stateside. I met Bob at Tarpon Springs, Florida, at our reunion in 1975 and would like to record a conversation we had.

Bob's family was well connected with the "Brass" in Washington, D.C. When he returned home they asked him why he was still a 2nd Lieutenant, after flying 50 tough combat missions – he must have goofed up! Bob blamed our Group C.O., saying, "No body gets promotions or medals". The "Brass" were angry, and said they would have our C.O.'s rear end back in Washington behind a desk! But Bob calmed them by saying, "Forget it – I'm home safe, it doesn't matter now."

It is disgustingly regretful that these high ranking "Brass", were the very people that caused all the trouble in the first place. For initially we flew under a Tech. Order list for 12 planes per squadron. When we went to 24 planes in early May '43, the Tech. Order remained the same. Many combat crew members from 1st Pilots to Gunners flew below the higher ranks they should have held – many were only Corporals. The same held for Ground Support men – I knew crew chiefs that never got above Buck Sergeants! We had flying Sergeants, Warrant Officers as pilots, enlisted men as Bombardiers, etc. Corporals and Privates as assistant crew chiefs! The most notorious morale breakers were the high "Brass" in Washington, D.C. – Not the German enemy!

There was one time in North Africa the Inspector General came to visit. We were told we could see him at any time about any complaints we had, but we couldn't complain about the food, or sleeping quarters. Heck, those were they only things we constantly complained about! So nobody visited the General.

There was one negative aspect affecting all personnel for many months. Someone was stealing morphine from the parachute packs. Each pack had an emergency kit to be utilized in emergency situations, when shot down or having to bail out of the plane in hostile territory. Area maps, a 10 dollar gold piece, fishing kit, waterproof matches, compass, etc., were part of the kit, plus various medicinal items…including morphine to treat the wounded. It was this vital item that was always missing from the emergency escape kit…morphine.

Every check, all safeguards, were implemented to account for this gross violation of Military ethics, and endangerment of our Air Crews lives. Extra guards were assigned to the planes, each crew member would ensure the morphine and all else were in the pack after a mission, and the chute packs were left at the various crew positions, all naively trusting to the integrity of all other men. But, in the morning…when crews came to fly the mission, a check of the packs showed the morphine was gone. The perpetrators were extremely clever for many, many months, and though suspicion lay heavily on two suspects…all investigation led to naught. No evidence was ever found to ascertain these, indeed, were the guilty parties. Procedures to protect the 'chutes were implemented to no avail…the morphine continued to disappear. So I must here recount my knowledge of the affair, which wouldn't end for over a year.

I had been a friend of one man, who also worked on the flight line. We went to town together whenever operations permitted. Many times I had gone somewhere with a squadron mate, not because we were good friends, but we were both alone, and happened to be headed in the same direction…so we hung out for that trip, and possibly other trips. Most of us chalked it up to coincidence.

One day suspect #1 and I were headed to Ain M'Lila separately, but subsequently visited the town together, simply because we were both headed that way. In walking down the main street, an Arab merchant beckoned my new friend into his store. We went to the back room while they spoke of something in French...which I neither spoke, or understood. On the wall, I watched them write 20,000...30,000 and other figures, not knowing what it all meant. Upon leaving the friendly Arab, I asked what all that was about, and my friend replied, "Oh, I want to sell him my mattress cover"! Well, it made sense to me... we had all been issued two mattress covers, and everybody I knew had sold one of their mattress covers to Arabs, as they were strong garments, one had only to cut a hole for the head, and 2 holes for the arms, and 'voila' the Arab had a good tunic to wear. GIs got 20 dollars for a mattress cover, so the above incident was nothing unusual, and I thought nothing more about it.

On another occasion, we went to Tunis, how that came about eludes me now, never the less, my friend went to an apartment, an expensive one, tiled vari-colored walls, mosaic fashion, with all the accouterments of a good fashionable domicile...even an Arab servant! We stayed overnight, separate bedrooms, and a servant who cooked and served breakfast. Again, I didn't think too much of it, as I knew a few of our officers had apartments in town, some being generous enough to let anyone use them, even enlisted men. I never felt any ulterior motive in #1's actions, at any time...I just thought he was a nice guy, and we got along good together, just as I did with others.

One day a good friend, who worked in the Intelligence section, approached me...Bob and I had been tent-mates and fine friends from the beginning days in Columbia, and my best friend in the squadron. Bob said I should keep away from #1. I became irritated at this, telling Bob that though we were good buddies, that didn't give him the right to tell me who to associate with. Bob then proceeded to tell me my life history, all about my schooling, family names, bits of information I know I never told him, resulting in my asking, "How in heck do you know all that"? Bob replied, "#1 is under investigation for the theft of morphine, and you are with him a lot, and you work on the flight line. You're a good friend, and I know you…I believe you are being sucked in as a dupe, to enhance his reputation, because he is hanging out with a good man…you! I'm trusting you to keep this quiet…I don't want you to get hurt". This was a total surprise, but I couldn't doubt Bob, he worked in S-2, Intelligence, the highest ranking enlisted man, and Capt. Nixon's right-hand man, and if he tells me, the C.I.D. is investigating me…then all the pieces as stated above, come falling into place. It was hard breaking the friendship with #1, as he had been an excellent friend, and all consequent excuses to him, as to why I didn't associate with him anymore, didn't even sound convincing to me. I didn't know how to lie, but I had to, and the lying made me feel guilty as hell. But I did manage to break it off. I have never been bothered by the fact I was investigated…the lies to #1 disturbed me more. Unfortunately, although #1 and #2 were watched continually, the thefts continued.

But by far the great and good men far outshone the bad. There were so many incidents of heroism, self-sacrifices and leadership that they were a daily occurrence, and would involve writing a book about them, which I have. I will offer one example here, as to the character of the great majority of Officers and men.

Our initial move to Italy, at landing at our new airfield, I told my Lt. Hart that if he knew of anyone going back to Tunis or Soliman, I had left my watch in a jewelers to be cleaned. My parents had scrimped and saved to buy the watch for my High School graduation gift. I thought no more about it as we were busy flying missions.

A few days later Lt. Hart came out to the plane and said, "let's take a ride Sarge". So we took off with me flying in the co-pilot position, not knowing whether we were going somewhere or just putting in flying time. As I pulled up the landing gear Hart tapped me on the shoulder, pointed to the stick, and yelled out compass direction. After flying on course for a long while, we hit Soliman airfield right on the nose. Upon landing he instructed me to stay in the airplane and headed for the tower. A few minutes later he drove up in a jeep. "Let's take a ride Sarge," and off we went. I figured we were going off somewhere to get supplies. But, as we entered Tunis he said, "Where is that jewelry shop, Sarge?" Can you imagine that? This guy taking his time off for me? And for a $30.00 watch! Nobody ever looked as big as he did then and never did I feel so humble – what a great gesture of friendship! Yes, I got the watch and I wore it with twice the pride, until it stopped working altogether many years later. It now reposes in an old cigar box, along with many fond memories of Joe Hart.

The 12th Air Force headquarters was located in Bari, Italy, consequently there were many vehicles parked around the barracks and headquarters buildings. There was very little transportation in our squadron. We decided to go to Bari and steal a jeep.

The "Jeep" had no ignition key – simply a built in switch on the dash one turned to the "on" position, hit the starter button on the floor, and "voila" – the engine was running.

Transportation was scarce, men had to walk to the "line" most of the time, and also hitch rides to Foggia or other destinations, so 3 unarmed individuals decided to rectify the situation and headed for Bari, the Headquarters of the Fifteenth Air Force, and also the busiest seaport on the Adriatic Sea.

In the blacked out night the men parked amid the hundreds of vehicles, lifted the hood of a brand new Jeep, put a new rotor in the distributor (rotors were removed to prevent anyone from using the Jeep, as stated above one didn't need an ignition key) started the engine, and left Bari for Amendola with the "appropriated" Jeep.

At the airfield the next morning the Jeep was subject to much battering with a sledge hammer, rocks and mud to make it look old, with appropriate squadron markings stenciled on the bumpers, we now had some needed transportation.

That night, the port of Bari was bombed by a sneak attack by the German Luftwaffe – the port was jammed with ships carrying cargo, waiting their turn to be unloaded. It was a second Pearl Harbor – 17 ships were sunk and 8 more damaged. The city of Bari was also bombed killing and injuring countless civilians. How lucky the three thieves were in choosing the time to steal a Jeep in Bari – they had been there the previous night.

As stated earlier we mechanics living out on the line, were a pretty independent bunch, not in isolation from others per se, but only wanting to be close to our own pride and joy B-25, consequently coming and going most anywhere without restriction, but yet adhering to Army Code and precepts the majority of the time.

Six of us took off one night for a house down the road where 3-4 Italian girls played many big band records of American music. There were 20 guys for every girl. Another GI we met there, a stranger to us, told us of a place in Battapaglia where we could have some fun...so we jeeped on down the road to the ruined city that had been our bombing target prior to the Salerno invasion. The city was in shambles, but a great many still lived there among the shattered buildings. We had our fun and returned to the base in the wee hours.

I was awakened at dawn by the 1st Sgt. I grouchily told him to let me sleep. He rapped me awake saying, "Sign this paper." I asked "what paper? I'll sign later." "Sign it now...there is no later," he demanded. After many expletives, I signed the paper and lay back to get more sack time. The 1st Sgt. Explained... "You and Davis were out last night, I have all the names. You stopped down the road, and one of the girls claimed she was raped by a soldier named Davis. By signing this paper, you have admitted to being AWOL, and accept company punishment for doing so. You can thank Captain Nipton for this...he saved you a court-martial." I was surprised and shocked, and very thankful for that wonderful Capt. Nipton...who else would have shown his trust and respect for us, as he did. No wonder everybody loved him! Our Davis had been with us all night...this we knew for a fact, and could prove it. But Nipton needed no proof…his belief in his men, prompted his actions to save his men trouble!

Sometime before I had been very surprised, when in standing at the club bar talking to one of our cooks, he put his arm around my waist and said, "You're mine". "You've got the wrong guy", I replied and moved down to the other end of the bar. I was shocked to know the cook was a homo! When upon my return from rest camp, I heard about a terrible beating afflicted by one man upon another, I was furious. The perverted crew chief who liked to get our new young recruits drunk, and beat them up, had beaten another man. I learned of the liaison between the cook and the battered man, and the perverted crew chief wanting the cook for himself. I vowed I would repay this guy, but could never get to him…I wanted to smash him silly for being the coward that he was.

Three crew chiefs and I were recommended for a Bronze Star for our planes having flown over one hundred missions without an early return. I knew this as fact, as two of my friends in S-2 and Operations had seen the papers, and had congratulated me, one even sending the notice to my local newspaper. Our engineering officer had to sign the papers, but wouldn't unless he got one also. He was told, "you have only been here two months, these men have been overseas nearly 2 years. But, he would not sign unless he was included. So we never received the award. It would have been nice to show the medal to my folks, but let's face it, there were more deserving men at the front, who had risked a hell of a lot more than I. At least, the pipsqueak Captain didn't get it.

Shortly before shipping overseas, I began to get K.P. and guard duty. This continued until the end of the war. As an assistant on my B-25, I didn't mind. When I became a crew chief and was assigned my own plane, the extra duty continued. A Crew Chief is probably the most important man in the maintenance of an airplane. He is the hands-on person who knows and is responsible for all that transpires, as to the airworthiness of the airplane. He makes the decision as to whether or not the plane is ready to fly. Be it a 2nd Lieutenant or a General, if the Crew Chief declares it isn't ready – that's it – it doesn't fly! So to take a Crew Chief away from his duty, for punishment duty unknown, without just cause, and never a hearing of any alleged wrong doing, is an insult, detrimental to the Combat Crews, and a morale breaker.

As the above punishment started in Louisiana, January 1943, the climax came at wars end as related below.

Add to that, the number of trips to various Mediterranean cities, Cairo, Tel-Aviv, Tripoli, Catania, etc, that were cancelled, that I was scheduled for as Flight Engineer, never going to rest camp for 2 years, all because of simple spite by one officer, to punish me for no reason, could have been demoralizing. After 2 ½ years of this stupid punishment of me, this was the boorish inane resulting confrontation, the day the war ended in Italy.

May 8, 1945, VE Day…and the day they 'gave the bar away'. Literally and actually…every man had at least 1 bottle of liquor…the medics even mixing batches of 200 proof alcohol to concoct various potent drinks. I had knocked off a fifth of Anisette, and was half way down on a bottle of Cherry Brandy.

There were a bunch of us in one room, all celebrating the end of hostilities. Captain Lord, 1st Sgt. Apperson, ex-first Sgts.; Matt Campbell, Hendrickson, Terhune, Line Chief Moe Martinez, Tony Furtivo and me. Feeling rather relaxed and happy, I asked Capt. Lord why he didn't like me. I told him he looked like a twin to my next door school chum back home, and I thought I had tried to be friendly with him. (I didn't mind being a friend of an Officer, but would never kiss anyone's fanny to do so.) He was surprised at my question and somewhat taken aback. This is approximately how the insipid, juvenile conversation went:

Renzi—"Would you mind telling me what I did wrong?"

Lord—"You know."

Renzi—"I don't know."

Lord—"You know."

Renzi—Beginning to feel frustrated… "I don't know, that's why I'm asking you."

Lord—"You know."

Renzi—Beginning to get angry, with no help from the liquor… "I asked a simple question, all I want is a simple answer."

Lord—"You know."

Renzi—Really losing my cool now… "I could get a better answer from a 12 year old…why won't you tell me?"

Lord—"You know."

Renzi—Angry now… "I asked what I've done wrong, and you sit there like a juvenile, saying "you know, …G--- D--- it…I don't know, quit acting like a kid and answer… you are supposed to be an intelligent officer!"

Lord—"You know…that letter you wrote."

Renzi—"What letter I wrote?"

Lord—"You know."

Renzi—Simmering now… "What letter I wrote, G---
D--- it!?"

Lord—"You know…that letter you wrote to your
Congressman!"

Renzi—"What letter I wrote to my Congressman?"
From way back in my mind a light is gradually growing
bright, and I remember suddenly of the incident in
DeRidder of my Dad informing me he would call his
Congressman to find out why I never got a furlough, way
back, a thousand years ago in January, 1943.

Capt. Lord sent Matt Campbell to the orderly room
for a letter he had sent to the Congressman, explaining
why…typical Army explanation, call of duty, etc. I read
the letter…and blew up!

"You rotten S.O.B.!...you mean you had this letter…
something I knew nothing about…and you didn't call
me in your office to inquire about it?" And for 2 ½
years you've been acting like a vengeful 10 year old kid,
shafting me with extra duty…getting even for something
I didn't do?" "Last one to get a plane…no rest camp for
2 years…no trips anywhere…you punk…you call yourself
an Officer?"… "You (I called him every rotten name in
the book)" and I headed for him…I was going to take him
out! Everybody jumped to hold me off him…and it took
everybody! I was never so raging mad in my life! That
broke up the party…and I was angry at all the 1ˢᵗ Sgts….
they must have known, but never told me. At least, if
I had known, I could have formally presented myself
to him, or my CO and had the misconception resolved
peacefully. To think he exacted revenge…revenge which
was more important than my primary loyalty to my
aircrews and plane!

The result – though 4 others and I had more than enough points to finally go home, after 3 ½ years in Service, we were sent to the Army of Occupation! Thank God for an understanding, fair minded Adjutant in our new outfit, the problem was resolved and we headed home. Because of the dumb officers I encountered in my term of Service, when asked to stay in the service, or the Reserves, I told them what they could do with the offer. Even though my life's dream was to become a Maintenance Officer in the Air Force, I declined. I knew that for the next 20-30 years I would run in to those types of inefficient dumb officers I had experienced in my time of service just completed. Thanks, but no thanks!!

The last incident of my service years was the "point system". Where to classify this, I'm not sure, but it belongs in the realm of ineptness, or morale breaking. These things were called SNAFU'S…Situation Normal, All Fouled Up!

When the Air activities ended in Italy, many replacements that had come into the squadron in the last year or so, were sent home to be assigned to the Pacific Theater of the War to help end hostilities there. That left all us old guys who had been in the Service from Day one, to maintain the planes and equipment, or to ready all for shipment back to the States. That's when the "point System" was announced!

One needed 85 points to go home, based on time in Service, time overseas, medals awarded, and other things long forgotten, but that was the gist of requirements. All the low point men had gone home, so we who had over 100 points were stuck overseas with all the planes and equipment and couldn't go home! It was later learned that all these low point men were still in the States when Japan surrendered, and never went to the Pacific, but instead were discharged, being some of the earliest men to get out of the service – and we were still overseas!

Eventually the "Brass" came up with an idea to transfer 10,000 high point men from the 12th Air Force, to the 15th Air Force, and the low point men from the 15th to the 12th. What disappoints me is, my Honorable Discharge says nothing of my 3 years in my Bomber Group, but instead reads that I was discharged from a P-51 outfit of the 15th Air Force! So much for my proud service to my B-25 Group and Squadron!

Though the previous incidents of inequities, whether moral, ethically, legally corrupt are but a few of nearly 4 years of Military service, they nevertheless show how acts such as those can affect the morale of one or many, in a tight cohesive first class unit in any branch of service.

Post WWII and the "same old same old" ---- --!

After leaving the Service in 1945 I had a few jobs in shipyards converting Victory ships, from troop carriers back to Cargo ships. Then took a job as a shipper in a well-known Chocolate factory. After a short time, one of my co-workers was promoted, and I was also, to take his job. Essentially the job was head shipper to the many stores owned by the company in the Big City, as well as many outlying stores in nearby States, in addition to volume jobbers in outlying states with national chains.

I visited the local chain of Chocolate shops, to make myself known rather than being a "telephone voice" taking orders for cartons of candy. On frequent occasions the company obtained small dolls or stuffed animals from overseas countries as novelties for customers, which I would send to each store in planned numbers. Eventually I would single out those stores that sold these items at a fast rate, and those that didn't do well, and allocate these items accordingly.

One day the owner approached me with a complaint from one store that they didn't receive as many items as other stores, asking me of the discrepancy. I told him I sent these imported toy items to the stores that were always asking for more, because they always sold out. The complaining store manager, never sold many, so sent back items unsold, which would have been sold at other stores, and I acted as any good businessman would.

I realized his warped intent, as everyone knew he was a very busy ladies man, with wearing very expensive clothes, form fitting top coat with a velvet collar, a homburg hat, silk scarf, tie with a diamond stick pin and yes – spats over his shoes! He cared less about his store sales, than he did his female store clerks.

But he didn't impress me, and if that's the way he wanted to operate, he could get someone else, so I quit. I had never gotten a raise for the added work and responsibility in over a year anyway. When I left two other men handled the job I did alone.

I went to work for my Brother-in-law as a mechanic, my first job as a mechanic since I left the Air Force 4 years earlier, and where at this period on my life I was to experience much in the way of police corruption – and again I emphasize, these things are considered normal.

A weekly occurrence at the garage was witnessing police cruisers stopping inside, and the cops telling my brother in law to take whatever he wanted. The cars would be full of goodies, the trunk also. Everything in the way of clothing items, from children's to adult's, all sizes, toys, household items, etc. There was always one of two cop cars every Friday without fail. Sometimes he would be asked if he needed anything in particular for the home! The reason for this?

The cops worked the same protection racket as the Mafia. The only difference being, to protect your business from robbers, thieves of any kind, a shop owner had to pay the Mafia protection money. With the cops it was, they would check your business all night to make sure you locked your doors, left a night light burning, secured any entrances. If you didn't reward them with these little goodies that you sold, whatever your business – they would not call you if your doors were unlocked, wouldn't call you – and maybe help themselves! Wouldn't even report to you if your store had been broken into! That's the answer to all the Friday night freebies! As my brother in law worked on cops private cars for nothing – well Friday was "Quid Quo Pro".

As to my initial complicity in corruption, working with my Brother in Law, there were really no facilities for cleaning myself up after a day in the garage, with the grease, oil, dirt and all else with being a mechanic I like to be clean, and felt enormously embarrassed in riding all the public transportation in my dirty clothes and person – so I bought my first used car to avoid feeling like a bum, as I worked many long hours, sometimes to early morning hours where public transportation ran once an hour.

During that time I was driving down a street that paralleled the main drag where one always had to wait behind trolleys or buses whenever they stopped, as there was never room to pass them, and was dangerous to do so anyway on that busy street – so we would go down the parallel street to get ahead of the trolley/bus as the parallel street came out on the main drag, a mile further on.

As I drove down that street, I soon came upon a horse and wagon delivering ice. Many people in those days couldn't afford a fridge so bought ice for their "ice chests" to keep the food fresh. The wagon was going about 1 or 2 miles per hour, so I gently nosed around him, at maybe 5 miles an hour, and immediately saw a cop standing off the curb about 3 blocks away. Driving about 10-15 MPH the cop flagged me down and started writing me up a ticket. I politely asked him why he was writing a ticket, and he replied, "For passing an ice wagon". I learned then, never dispute a cop in any way – most will be easier on you, the less you say. Instead I took the ticket, made a beeline to a bar where a friend of my Brother, who I also knew, was working part time as a bartender. His full time job was a local cop. I told him my problem – we both knew there was no law against passing a wagon. Soon the cop who wrote the ticket came into the bar, through the efforts of my brother's friendly bartender. The cop/bartender talked to him a minute, came down to where I was sitting, and said "Buy him a drink, he'll tear up the ticket". So for a drink of booze, I saved myself paying a fine, and my driving record. I'm sure that is the one and only time I did something like that, and it has always bothered me that I was no better than the corrupt people I came to despise. But again, it is the Quid Pro Quo, something for something, so prevalent in our society today, from the smallest to the biggest. The ticketing of me was to make an example of me for other motorists.

While working at this time, television was new and expensive, too much so for me to afford one. So I would go to a bar to watch the Friday night fights, which at that time was as popular as Monday night football is today. One bar I went to often was owned by one of the most famous Flyweight Champions of the world, who gained fame through 3 fights in New York's Madison Square Garden. And this was the place where the Friday night fights were that we saw on television. In the bar, and usually right in front of the television would be what we called the "Suits". The "Suits" got that name from being in the Mafia, and wearing suits that cost in the minimum 400-500 bucks. This in an era where ordinary guys and I bought suits for 50 dollars on the installment plan – like 2 dollars a week!

One particular fight was between an up and coming fighter, either a lightweight or middleweight, against a well known journeyman, who you had to beat in order to get ranked for a shot at the title. The young comer was Charlie Fusari. He was supposed to take a dive, and lose the fight. Instead he walloped the journeyman, and won the fight – but he was never seen again! We learned all this through the Mafia "suits", knowing the fight was fixed the Mafia guys bet on the supposed to win journeyman. Of course they were furious when Fusari won – he won a one-way ticket to oblivion! The Great Middleweight Rocky Graziano even writes of taking a dive when told to do so – or else!

When I was first married, my wife was Italian, in the same town as above. Her Dad was a great guy, quiet, unassuming, just a nice person. One afternoon he asked me if I would like to go to a bar, near the bar above, for a couple of beers. He wasn't a drinker per se, and so I accepted his unusual invitation. While sitting at the bar conversing, this big burly guy came over from a table in the corner, gave my father in law a big hug, kissed him on both cheeks, with a big "hello, how are ya" and was very pleased to see us. I was introduced to him, and he came over to me and whispered to me, "You're his son in law, that's good enough for me – any time you want someone's legs broken, just come and see me! I'll kill ya mudder for nuttin!" After a few minutes he returned to his table, and a few minutes after that another big behemoth came over and repeated much the same big hug and all that the former fellow has said and done. Again I was introduced to this second guy, who slapped me on the back, almost busted my hand in shaking hands with me, and like his buddy, said the same thing to me as his buddy did, except he said, "I'll kill ya mudder for fi dollars" - he was a bit more expensive! All this with much cursing and offensive cuss words!

The reason? My Father in law was an insurance man, sold insurance to families, and like milkmen, newsboys, laundrymen, and many other tradesmen, came to all the houses on their routes every week to collect money for their services – all this was common practice during the Great Depression era. My Father in law was a giving, caring person, had a steady job and good income, and knew these hometown people for years. So if someone were out of work and couldn't pay the weekly premiums on the policies they had for the whole family individuals, that cost anywhere from 5-10-15 cents each, he would pay out of his own pocket, rather that see the policies on the kids lapse. These two Mafioso never forgot his goodness. Though my Father in law never took money or anything else, just being a good caring neighbor the people remembered – hence my inclusion as a Mafia friend.

About 5 years later his company learned of his kindness in doing this for others, and this honest goodhearted man, after 30 years of labor, was fired. It literally broke his heart – he took to drinking, retreated into his shell, broken and ashamed, he died too young. After years of keeping others afloat, he died for being a big, caring, goodhearted person. Sometimes the reward for goodness is badness – provided by those who have no moral courage themselves.

A few years later my marriage broke up. There were numerous times I would be called to court, as my ex wanted more money. They were already taking 2/3's of my pay for support. I only had money to pay my board and commute to work. In attempting to speak to the judge about visitation rights to see my child, I was always told by the Judge, "I don't want to hear a thing, just send the money"! Never was I heard, as children are always used as a tool by wives without justification, against their husbands, denying the kids access to their Dads – the wives get revenge – the kids get rotten lives. I don't wonder way some guys take off for parts unknown and are never heard from again – what a shame – instead of being judicious the courts are judgmental! Eventually the courts got tired of the constant appearances, and cut my payments to give me breathing room.

There was a new Commissioner of State Public Works Department. I decided to go see him. He was a friend of my Dad's. Using my Dad's name I asked his receptionist if I could see him. When I went into his office he said "you're not Jimmy". I said, "No, I'm his son, he has no idea I'm here, I didn't think you would know me, I need a job". I told him my experience, a verbal resume if you will. He told me never to use my Dad's name again in the way I did, it wasn't right, and I apologized for that.

He made a phone call, and I heard him discussing the creation of a job for me, at a figure nearly twice what I had made heretofore! I was happy and amazed at my good fortune and connection. Soon after another man came to the office, and much whispering went on. That new job creation was nixed by this other person, and, instead of my having the job I expected, I got a job as a General Cleaner of the shop. A menial job, but never the less I had work and that was important.

In talking to my Dad later on, I learned the reason I hadn't gotten the new job being created for me, was that the Commissioners flunky had been friends for years, and about 20 years prior, the flunky and my Dad had a falling out, when my Dad worked for Public Works during the Depression, and so he immediately was against anything I did. But he couldn't hold me back, I was an excellent mechanic, and soon became a top mechanic due to my solving a couple of problems on trucks. I worked for the State for 12 years, and in all those years, no matter what I did, nothing was good enough for the flunky, who had become my supervisor. All State jobs were Civil Service jobs, and one had to sign papers for a job, and wait your turn until a job opening occurred in your occupation. It wasn't until after I was given the job, when I applied for it and got my name on the Civil Service list. Again a wrong approach, but as I say, "it isn't what you know, but who you know", that counts. The longer I worked there, I came to realize all my co-workers had gotten their job the same way – through connections, most of the connections were politicians. I at least didn't pay for my job, and I don't hesitate to say, I was a top man, and the only man to get a letter of commendation for my work – the 1st award ever given. So yes, a morally or ethical wrong way to get a job, but I gave back ten fold.

In my early days on the above job, I would occasionally help out as a 3rd man when it was necessary to pick up a piece of highway machinery such as bulldozers, or rollers, graders, etc., that must be moved to a new location, or coming to the shop for overhaul.

The regular helper on that lowboy trailer had ambitions to be a cop, and eventually, through his own political connections he got a job as a Police officer. His first day on the job he came running into the shop, laughing and hollering, waving a 5 dollar bill in his hand, shouting "Look! Look! My first one!" That's why he wanted to be a cop, to make money shaking down "motorists"!

There was another guy worked in the shop as a general cleaner. He had been a well-known professional fighter. He also wanted to be a cop, and so through his political connections, he was placed on the police force in the big city. He was what we called "punchy", taking too many punches to the head. But they made him a cop anyway.

Not long after his appointment he was making a purchase in a liquor store, being off duty and out of uniform. A young kid came into the liquor store to commit a robbery. He collected all the money and ran to the door – at which point the punchy fighter/cop pulled his gun and emptied it into the kids back – 6 times he was shot, and every one in the back! I don't know the outcome of that case, probably punchy is sitting home enjoying his pension.

I've always loved Big Bands and jazz, and went to see them and various jazz musicians at different venues, many times with my brother who is also a jazz afficionado.

We went to one illegal after-hours club to attend a jam session in which a couple of Duke Ellington's musicians were appearing. When we got to the club, there was a police sergeant walking around outside near the entrance, and so we stalled around hoping he would leave, and we could then get into the club. But he never left the area, and after 15 minutes or so, he called out to us, "Hey, are you waiting to get into the club? If you are, I got the keys!" So we walked over and he unlocked the door saying, "Have a good time"! Another payoff to the cop, by the club owners.

The reason people enjoyed after hours jam sessions, was that in playing in a big band setting, most music was arranged, and one couldn't express himself, or show off his talents. At jam sessions, he could really let go musically, and show how good he could play, and the people loved these improvised sessions.

We used to frequent another after hours club in the big city. I well remember my first time. I pulled my car parallel to the curb to park. Immediately a police sergeant started yelling at me for parking the normal way. He screamed, "Get that car out of there and park it right! Angle it in to the curb so we can get more cars in here"! Cops were a helpful bunch!

In those days before I played music in clubs, we went to small clubs where there was a piano player and an open mike, and anyone could get up to sing whatever he/she liked, sober or not. It was always a fun nite.

One night while enjoying the music and singing, about 8 cops came in the club, and we didn't have an idea of what was happening, with 4 cops in the club lounge, and 4 cops on the separated bar side of the club. We heard the bartender shouting and cursing the cops and we wondered at the commotion. Soon the bartender hollered to the cops, "I'm calling the owner, you can fight with him"! Soon the owner showed up, and he was angry as all get out, cursing at all the cops, telling them to get out of his club! He screamed, "I pay the Captain at the station, I pay the Lieutenant in this area, I pay the Sergeant, and I pay all the cops on the beat! You guys are getting nothing! And if you don't get the f--- out, I'm calling the station, and they'll get you out!" After that ranting and raving by the club owner, the 8 cops left the club.

As we learned, the 8 cops were from another jurisdiction in the big city, they didn't belong there, and wanted a fifth of liquor for each of them. It was nothing more than an attempted "shakedown" of the club owner that didn't work, as he was already paying off the local cops, for whatever eventuality that may occur, and would require help from the local police. A pretty commonplace thing in the city.

It was pretty well known by most people that the Mafia owned or controlled most of the clubs in one way or another – especially the big name clubs where stars of stage and screen would appear, from Sinatra, Billy Eckstine, Jerry Vale, Connie Francis, and so many, many more of that day, so we occasionally went to those clubs also. Many Mafioso worked in the clubs, as waiters, Maitre De's, bouncers, and so on. They weren't the ideal first class people, some butchered the language, or were very inept in their jobs – but they belonged to the mob in one way or another, so it was pretty common to see these people working in the clubs.

My brother was in the merchant marine, and sometimes between trips, would take time off, to visit New York or some other place. He made a few trips to Florida to visit the Red Sox, as we both had friends who worked for the team. On one trip he met a girl who worked for Ringling Bros. Circus and became good friends, as the circus trained in the same town as the Sox.

One ship he worked on made weekly round trips to England from New York. While in London he had an expensive suit and topcoat custom made for him, which he showed off and telling of its expensive cost. While home he went to this famous nite club to see one of the stars of that day, and saw the girl from the circus, so they hugged each other like good friends do – and immediately was jumped by mafia goons, who stomped him to the floor, tearing his topcoat and suit to shreds. That's the way these goons work – shoot first and ask questions afterward. Of course they never apologized or paid for my brothers clothes either! She also happened to be a girlfriend of the Mafioso!

I also knew a friend who was employed by the mafia in their "counting house" – the backroom where the bookies turned in all the money people bet on numbers, horses and dogs. He had worked for the Mafia for a number of years, but like a lot of people he got greedy. He just couldn't bear counting all that money without dipping into it. So they caught him skimming, a bit here, a bit there – and they fired him, which was lucky for him, as they could have really hurt or killed him. Instead they got him a job in the post office, and he had to repay all the money he took, to the mafia.

I was at his house one time, when he had a visitor. They went into the living room and were sitting at a table alone talking softly. I had to pass the living room to get to the kitchen, and in doing so, noticed a gun on the table, and heard the Mafioso say, "Look buddy, you're the guy that screwed up, not me. They sent me here to tell you to pay up or else! It's up to you"! I never inquired one way or another about my friends problem, and have no idea of the outcome, as I had come west shortly after that.

As stated before, most people I worked with got their job because of who they knew, whether it is family, friend, friend of a friend, that is common practice in this country, and is the main reason all government entities, everywhere are so inept, for you don't have to know your job, you just need a connection to get the job, and you're in!

I worked with a guy who came in everyday, well dressed, punched his time card, took off his outer clothes, put on a smock and his homburg, and walked out the gate. He wouldn't return till closing time, go through the same thing as before and punch out his time card. After one of the most famous armored car heists in history, he was never seen again. Another missing man from the same heist, was the uncle of one of my fellow co-workers!

Probably the most blatant of all abuses of political connections I have ever known about, is the story of the mechanic who worked in the truck stall next to me, where we overhauled all the trucks every spring and summer.

He came in one day all agitated and hyper. I could tell he was eager to unload whatever he had on his chest, just dying to tell someone something. He approached me a few times ready to unload whatever it was, then would change his mind. Every time he did this piqued my curiosity even more, and I decided to wait and whatever was agitating him would come out.

Finally after a few hours he came over to me and said, "We did it!" I looked at him, and said, "Did what? What happened". Very excited and nervously agitated, he blurted out the whole story.

He and a buddy got drunk one night, and being out of their skulls, drove up the wrong side of a divided highway. They collided with another car head on, and killed an elderly couple. His politician State Senator, got together with the judge hearing the case, paid the judge 3000 dollars, and the two drunken bums were let off scott free!! This stupid fool actually felt relieved to have finally told someone – I personally think he was somehow bragging how they had gotten away with murder.

Some years later after I had come west, I made a visit to the shop to see my old friends, some who were still there after twenty some years. I was surprised when they told me to visit the Superintendent of the shop, to see who the new guy was. I walked into the office, and lo and behold! Sitting there as big as life is the guy who caused the death of two old people, my ex-mechanic friend. There's nothing that corrupt people, especially corrupt politicians can't do!! And to think this state senator later sat in Washington, D.C., as a member of Congress!!

There are 3 final incidents I would like to mention relating to my time in my home state. All differ in nature but are worth the mention, especially one dealing with a very special friend.

In the early 50's it was election time, and I read of one person who was running for the Head School Committees office in the big city. He spent an inordinate amount of money for the job, close to 200,000 dollars, a lot of money in those days. And I was perplexed. Why would anyone spend 200,000 bucks for a job that paid 1 dollar a year. Yup, you heard it right! I read about it in the main Big City newspaper, as it was raising other eyebrows. Inquiring around, and knowing there was no school construction going on, or planned, I met someone more knowledgeable than I, and he told me there was more money to be made in "school supplies", than anywhere else in city government. Under the table of course!

When I first started working on the job mentioned above as a mechanic, I was approached by another of my politically connected co-workers. He asked me if I had been in the service and if I received any pension from my service. I told him I was acknowledged to have had an injury; but was awarded "more than zero, but less than 10 percent" – which meant I got no pension for my injury. He told me to go to the V.A. and ask for a certain guy, and do whatever he told me to do. I did so, met this person, was escorted down a side corridor, into an elevator, up a couple of floors, exited the elevator into an office suite of the head of the V.A. I told him of my injury overseas, filled out some papers, and a few weeks later, received 10 percent disability payment. I paid no one nothing. For years the money went to my Mom, who only got the lowest social security payment, for she had never paid into it – she was married with 8 kids, so never worked to contribute to the system. I have only had the disability pension since my Mom passed away. I'm glad it helped her!

One reason I accepted the V.A. 10 percent pension at that time was that I had other veterans ask me about the same thing, and would laugh and deride me, as they were getting as much as 60% disability for athletes foot – and hadn't even been overseas! That irked me.

Another item of connections experienced by me. I flatly state – that with the exception of buying a cop a drink for tearing up a ticket, I have never given anyone a thin dime, or did a favor for any person, except 2 politicians who got me a job when I was desperate for a job to support my family – all I promised was to vote for them. And I figured if they did something worthwhile for me or any constituent, I would at least give them my vote for a much needed job.

Another thing one did for me was to alert me to a veterans program every town has. There is a Veterans fund one can get money from in an emergency, something I never knew. I availed myself of this program to pay all my back bills, that grew weekly while unemployed. One stipulation – you had to pay it back, so other veterans could also access the program, and it was only an honor system, they wouldn't chase you for the money, only depended on your integrity. I paid back every cent, though it hurt financially at the time, more than my injured back!

After a few years I was told to see a V.A. doctor for re-evaluation – which at that time was a government ploy to take pensions away from the vets. Through another connection I went to see a certain V.A. doctor, who in asking me questions about my injury, shook her head yes or no, as to how to answer the questions. I didn't lose my pension. The reason – the doctor was being transferred to Washington, D.C., and had sole care of her 80 some year old mother, who would have been alone, no relatives being in her area. Through a mutual connection, she was allowed to stay where she was, the transfer never happened. To repay her connection, she would do favors, like the favor for me, to our mutual connection. How did I get this connection? I knew the family for years, having been their home delivery newsboy for many years as a youngster. That's it!! Quid pro quo!

Main item #2 is to give you an idea how some people work with their connections.

Just before I came west, I started my attempt to play jazz harmonica in a few clubs. I went to visit my brother, who introduced me to Bobby Hackett whom I referred to at the beginning of this book. After enjoying Bobby's trumpet and cornet playing, his pianist, famous in his own right, for his pianistic expertise, who plays at many jazz festivals, etc., went to my brother's house, along with another pianist and a bass player. The pianist, who I'll call Al, was already feeling no pain, having guzzled 2 fifths of vodka while playing at the club.

My brother suggested Al and I playing a few things in his den. So we went to the den and commenced to play. Halfway through the song Al started to play with his elbows, crashing down on dozens of notes, sounding like a little kid banging on the piano keys. I felt pretty miffed, and I stopped playing, and said, "I don't need this crap from you or anyone". I walked out to the kitchen, everyone following. The other pianist, Bob, and the bass player were very angry to see me treated this way by this famous Al, and they let him know in no uncertain terms how they felt about his treatment of me, famous name or not.

The bass player said to Al, "Let me tell you a little story Mr. Bigshot. Just because you think a harmonica isn't a legitimate instrument, and music is his favorite hobby, and because he is a mechanic, let me tell you something. I'm a bass player, but my main job is a plumber. That doesn't mean we don't know or love music. We give our best, and you should respect the fact we spend all our spare time learning to play jazz!"

The plumber went on, "I'm gonna tell you a true story, and you better listen hard. One time I was working in a club with a six piece group. We worked all night, and at the end of the night, the group leader went up to the club owner to get paid for all the musicians. The club owner said, "Everyone gets paid except the bass player – he stinks"! The band leader said it didn't matter that he didn't like the bassists playing, he worked all night and should be paid. The club owner insisted he wouldn't pay the bass player, and they argued to and fro for quite awhile, all the while the club owner using choice expletives concerning the bass player. Finally the bass player said, "I'm going to ask you nicely one last time, I'm sorry you don't like my playing, but I worked all night and should get paid like the rest of the guys." The smart alec club owner replied in every expletive word, "If you don't get out of here I'm going to throw your expletives out thru that door." The bass player said, "OK guys, I tried," and the band left.

The next morning the club owner went to the club, and all he saw was a pile of ashes, the club burned down.

About the time the shocked club owner could say a word, the bass player walked up to him and said, "Now do I get paid?"

The bass player had mafia connections. And so after that above story, the bass player and Bob left my brother's house, and I too said good night and walked out. Waiting outside were Bob and the bass player. They said, "we're waiting for that mother to leave, and we're gonna break every one of his fingers so he'll never play again. It was then that I realized they were both mafia guys! I don't exaggerate when I say it took me over an hour, that he wasn't worth it, it would be a waste of time, and might be trouble. You better believe they would have broken all Al's fingers and maybe much more. Another lesson in not getting too close, or opposed to mafia figures!

Now I come to a factual story that is clear to my heart. Not because of the corruption involved, as that was pretty prevalent in my life. It is very clear because I am a personal friend of the man in this story and know much about what was related to me. He is the most dedicated, heroic man I know or have ever known, and yet I know little of his ordeal, either in his WWII years, or his battle with corrupt forces. As in previous accounts in this narrative, I have eliminated real names, as of this late date, I don't want to open a Pandora's box, or can of worms, that may hurt many people, I have no axe to grind, nor any rewards to reap, except to hopefully open eyes that have been closed too long, brains that have been comatose, and people like me who have felt helpless too long.

I'll call my friend "Lou". I first met Lou in the 4th grade so many years ago, and about the same time met one of my female classmates, who eventually married Lou, to raise a family and were happily married until she passed away. Both were genuine friends, though I didn't see them very often as shortly after WWII I married and moved to another town.

Most of the events surrounding Lou I've heard many years later as Lou very seldom talks about the bad things in his life, and not in great detail. I have to fill in some of the blanks.

Lou enlisted in the U.S. Marines shortly after Pearl Harbor. I do know he became a drill instructor at Paris Island, S.C., and then went to the Pacific. Whatever went on in that period I don't know. But I do surmise it had to be heroic, for he was sent to Officer's Candidate School at Quantico, Va., and became a 2nd Lieutenant. Again he doesn't talk about where he was or what he did, but again must have done some very worthwhile deed somewhere and probably was promoted to 1st Lieutenant. And then had to come some other brave action, for when he went into Iwo Jima, he was a Captain, commanding a company of men. All I know is when he came off the island after it's surrender, there were only 40 men left of his company. He says one of our childhood friends died in his arms on the beach.

Over the years he tells me only bits of information about Iwo, as only 2 years ago he told me that after 60 years of hating the Japs he finally stopped that feeling. The little bit of his exploits and what I have read over the years, helps me understand his feelings, and that they came from the horrendous atrocities Japanese troops perpetrated on our dead and wounded Marines during the battle for the island.

Even his experiences as a police officer are few, and years between the telling. He is the most honest person I have ever met, and I am proud to be his friend. So his story as brief, and the bits and pieces told to me over the years, tells me that his heroism didn't end at Iwo Jima.

He received a football scholarship at college and majored in English, and I wish I had his descriptive writing ability! So following his WWII service he joined the local police force, much of what is written about on preceding pages.

One nite he made a stop on a car that had failed to stop at the required "stop sign". The guys in the car were all former classmates who's names he won't tell me, but knowing what I do I have a good idea of who they are. They were all now fringe mafia, bookies, numbers men, runners, etc. They told him to tear the ticket up, as they could have it fixed anyway. Being an honest cop, friend or no, Lou refused to tear up the ticket. From that measly 5 dollar ticket, the incident was blown all out of proportion, in the mafia's attempt at revenge. What ensued was 2 years of punishment for Lou for writing that ticket.

Lou was put on a night waterfront beat, and for 2 years had to endure all sorts of weather, winter being the worst in those days, with the many blizzards sweeping the area. He told me one time, he had to ring in his call box in a limited time frame, and if he was a minute late he would get extra duty.

In the freezing weather, thigh high snow, he trudged along the waterfront. He said to me, "Every step I took in those 2 years, I would say repeatedly, "Someday I'll get those sons-of-bitches", over and over."

After the 2 years they relieved him of that torturous duty, and for some strange reason, I can't figure yet – they put him on the Vice Squad!!?

And did he proceed to go to town! He arrested anyone and everyone connected with booking horses, the numbers games. He had his own group of informers who tipped him to illegal card games and gambling.

The cop who fixed my traffic ticket was caught, in uniform, dealing the highest stakes card game in town, and was tossed off the force. He never talks about it, but he went through that town like a whirlwind in his vendetta to those who had punished him unlawfully. Most of what happened in those days, I read about in Newsweek Magazine, and I couldn't believe the mafia would do something like that to Lou.

They threatened to blow up his house, kill his wife and kids – all sorts of evil things were made known to Lou and his family. But Lou wouldn't back down. There were court cases after court cases, all resulting in meager 25 or 50 dollar fines against the mafia errand boys. How are you going to scare a guy that survived all the Pacific war had invoked? I can't remember how long this went on – but it was a long time. It was similar to what Ralph Nader experienced when he blew the whistle on General Motors. I doubt they scared Lou – I'm sure he scared them – you don't mess with truly honest people!

I met Lou one day as he was leaving the Big City Courthouse. We exchanged bear hugs, and he said to me, "My friend, I'm glad it's over, this was the last case. What surprised me was how naïve I was, I thought all cops were honest, that's why I joined the force". And I said, "Lou that's the very reason I never joined, when my Dad suggested it after I came back from the war. I told my Dad that in order to be a cop, you had to be a crook, and that is the only time my Dad didn't argue with me".

I only saw Lou once or twice being involved in my own problems. Then when I came west, and made visits to Lou and his wife, he would mention something about his travails of these times.

Years later he told me of a day when he had just left for work. The doorbell rang, and when his wife answered, there was one of our classmates, and so being as cordial as we all were in those days, Lou's wife invited the guy in, and offered him breakfast, and turned to get him a cup of coffee. When she turned around there was a 45 caliber gun lying on the table, and our classmate said, "Don't you think you ought to tell Lou to back off?"

He also told me of the day we met at the Big City courthouse, on his last court case. He tells me he went back to the station house, picked all his police stuff from his locker and left. He says he got dirty looks, and rotten comments from the cops as he left. I have seen all his equipment, badge, gun, etc.

He never quit – he was never fired – they just forgot he ever existed. Lou is the greatest guy I ever met, and will always be a hero in my mind – and the most honest man I ever met!

We still visit, E-mail, talk and will always be great friends!

To close out my years in the east, it is only fitting to mention one figure who may have been as corrupt as any politician, receiving money and favors from special interest, but acted in a much different manner than others. A motion picture was made of his life.

The man had been the Mayor of the Big City for a number of terms. He also served as Governor of the state for many years. And was elected to the U.S. Congress, the total spanning all of his adult life.

From all accounts I have read about, or have been told to me by people who were well acquainted with the man, however the knowledge came, all relate similar accounts of the goodness of the man. He was portrayed as the modern "Robin Hood" – he took from the rich, and gave it to the poor. There also was a song of that title.

People told of the depression days, and the hardships, with no jobs, kids to feed, no money and plenty of bills, the embarrassment of being on welfare, the freezing winters.

And they told of the countless times they called this man, because there was no heat in the house, and they would call him, and very shortly, a truck would be there with a load of coal for the furnace. Or the very many times, the families in dire need of food would call him, and the immediate reply from him was a carload of groceries to feed the starving kids. I don't know the number of people helped by this man in his lifetime, or the many other charitable works he performed, but he was a legendary figure throughout the state.

I don't know the personal story of many of our great men, every where in the world, but their exploits are known and passed down by others, and so we understand the legacy of these men, good and bad.

Evidently this now Congressman must have made enemies, for whatever reason, and was indicted, convicted, and imprisoned for tax evasion. Even though in prison, he was elected to Congress again by the people. He was much loved by those he helped in their need, and of those who knew of his goodness of helping others.

The circumstances of his death, are long forgotten by me, as to his passing away while still incarcerated. But nevertheless, what was important to all was his wealth. Most people thought, that with the decades of long government service, he had to be at least a millionaire, perhaps multi. But when his will was published his assets were, his home, and a 90,000 dollar bank account! He had truly given away all the bribes the lobbyist had bestowed upon him for expected favors.

I have seen funerals of heroes, presidents, and of the famous men in my time, but nothing like the funeral of this man. Everyone took the day off, streets were crowded with people, mourning and crying as the motorcade wound through the city. I had never seen such a turnout of mourning people in my life, and haven't since.

I have to ask – was this really a corrupt man, or did he make corrupt practices work for the people? He was an old man when he died, but I don't doubt he left youngness of heart with those he aided in their time of need.

PERSONAL EXPERIENCES

There were about 8 women I was involved with over a period of time, whom I won't talk about, with one exception. In all cases but one, the first cheated for 2 years, and when I dumped her, she married the guy. The second was really the worst though she never cheated. The 3rd was a hidden closet druggie and cheater, the fourth also cheated at least twice, as I caught her both times, fifth was an alcoholic and also used drugs, 6th was a liar and never told the truth, though she didn't know I knew all about her. Number seven was a closet hooker, and I wouldn't doubt was bi-sexual.

The second was the most miserable of anyone I have ever met. We saved together and bought a house, used to visit it on weekends, to observe the stages of construction, looking forward to moving in with all new furniture in a nice newly constructed development. It would be good to leave the city and its 100 year old tenements. With a brand new son we finally went to our new home, a week after he was born.

Upon entering the house my wife exclaimed, "I hate it, I'll always hate it, sell it!!" Shocked and surprised, I could only say, "What do you mean you hate it, we just bought it"? She continued to say how much she hated it, and to sell it! I was taken aback and confused. Her savings were the down payment, my savings were for the new furniture – I had worked 2 jobs for what I thought would be a good and happy life, she and I both signed all the necessary papers, so this outburst was totally out of the blue.

At the time, I thought maybe our son had something to do with it, but really didn't know. This was years before someone came up with the idea of post-partum depression.

Needless to say, she worked at hating the new home, went to bed and stayed there for 2 weeks, while I used up all my sick leave to take care of our newborn. I fed him, bathed, and did all I could to alleviate the situation to no avail. In fact, I fed him breakfast for 4 years, made my own lunches before leaving for work.

No matter what I did in enhancing the house, or property, gardening, building a recreation room, nothing satisfied her. Neighbors invitations for coffee klatches, were ignored, she hated the neighbors and the neighborhood. I could have tripled or quadrupled my income by working over time, or going on the road during the week, which would have done wonders and relieved much of the financial burden, which was only a week-to-week existence. Working overtime was out, it only led to prolonged arguments, which were a daily occurrence anyway. I had a neighbor woman who told my wife, "I can set my clock by the time your husband gets home everyday". I never "stopped off" with my co-workers for a beer or two, as they did occasionally – marriage was more important, and especially the way things were at home. The guys thought I didn't like them!

The upshot of all these 4 years — I was asked by my foreman to go on the road to the furthest district to maintain the equipment during all the blizzards, to keep the roads open. I had done this for years previous to my 2nd marriage, knew all the personnel and the area and maintenance procedures, but told my foreman I didn't think my wife would like me on the road. He said it was only for 2 weeks, as my buddy, who took over when my wife didn't want me on the road, or working overtime, had a wife who was sick and I was the only man he could depend on to do the job. I told him I'd do my best but doubted I could change my wife's mind.

Naturally, the initial approach was rebuffed by my wife. I told her it would only be for 2 weeks, and I would be home the first week end. Besides that Christmas was 2 weeks away and we sure could use the extra money. The money clicked in her mind for the first time in 4 years.

Telling my foreman of the OK for 2 weeks, I got a new truck, and as noted previously, I played the 4 number plate numerals on the trucks license plates for 25 cents, I hit for 250 dollars! Wow! What a bonus that would be for Christmas!

We made out a Christmas list of both families, excluding nobody, with the 250 dollars. I bought what I thought was a beautiful imported bracelet, with dangling baubles, with beautiful filigreed figures, all in solid sterling silver, for my wife's Christmas present.

The first week I quadrupled my take home pay, worked 18-20 hours a day. The second week I tripled my pay, and was satisfied to have earned all that money, and that no job was left unfinished.

We went to visit her folks, and then mine, gift giving being especially joyful for the first time in 4 years. We received a lot of nice gifts, my wife more so, as my sisters never skimped in gift giving, and so my wife was the recipient of their largess. I was pretty happy driving home.

When we entered the house, my wife exclaimed furiously, "Why don't they give me the money instead of this stuff!!" And she threw the bags all over the kitchen floor! How quickly the happiness I felt was turned to disgust with this latest outburst – that was the straw that broke this camels back!

I told her, "I've had it! I've listened and watched your selfishness for 4 years – nothing I, or anyone else does for you satisfies you! I've put up with enough, when I come off the road I'm seeing a lawyer!!"

I left the house, drove around aimlessly, knowing I couldn't go this abnormal marriage any longer – I was forever shoveling crap against the tide, banging my head against a brick wall – I'd really go nuts trying to live a good and decent life with this anchor around my neck!

After doing my best to calm down, and think rationally – I was told that I'd have to work on the road till the end of the season, another 3 months, as my buddy's wife was still sick. I let my wife know, and told her the job was important, as we needed the money, and I could work overtime only in the winter months. Like it or not, it was settled. My bosses depended on me, and I depended on my job performance to take care of home responsibilities. About that time I asked my wife for 10 dollars for a pair of dress shoes, as I hadn't bought myself anything in 8 years. She said she had no money! I said, "I've given you nearly 600 dollars in 2 weeks, and you don't have any money?" She repeated the "no money" reply, and I decided from then and there – I would never again put my check or pay on the table. It would be in my pocket!!

I finished my stint on the road, with an excellent letter of commendation for the Chief Engineer of the district for the outstanding work I and my assistant had done – the first letter of commendation ever given to anyone in my department since day one! In later showing the letter to my Dad, he remarked, "It won't buy you a cup of coffee"! And no matter the cursory remark – he was right – it never has!

In talking to my buddy one day, I noticed his flashing a new watch and immediately knew where it came from. And so I said to him, "Tips must have been good"! He knew that I knew where the watch had come from. His wife hadn't been sick – he was going with the waitress in a beer joint we went to for lunch! He didn't want to go on the road because of her! My long friendship with him dropped a thousand notches. But I didn't blame him for my troubles – those had been there long before I went on the road.

I began to notice a car parked outside the shop, where no parking was allowed on that main road, and in looking in my rear view mirror saw that he seemed to be following me. I had observed a couple of things before that, but hadn't paid much attention. This time I decided to find out who this was. So I stopped at a gas station, bought a pack of smokes, noticed the same car, parked 50 yards below the station, then drove off, stopped at a store for a newspaper, saw the same car parked a little way, knew he was following me, so proceeded to give him a tour of the countryside, to roads I'd never been on before, and finally shook him off and went home. I was later to learn, my wife or in-laws had hired this guy, figuring I had a girl friend!

One day I came home from work, walked in to the house – and it was completely empty! Not a thing left, except my clothes closet being emptied, and what little clothes I had, strewn all over the floor!

The following weekend I saw my son, and wife, now living with her folks, paid her for my son's keep, and did that for 3 weeks, in cash, mentally reminding myself to give her a check or money order from now on.

A couple of days later, the shop loudspeaker, summoned me to the office. I reported to the Superintendent, and asked did he call me. He replied, "This officer wants to see you". I turned around and there was a police officer standing there. I asked, "What happened, is my wife and son ok?" He didn't know, so I asked what was going on, did something happen at home – what was he there for. He said he didn't know, only I had to report to the station in my town.

"Can I wash up or change clothes,"? He said ok, and I hurried to the washroom, him following behind. I said, "I'll be right there, you don't have to follow" – but he did anyway, me wondering what had happened, and his strange behavior, for he watched me wash, change clothes, and when I said I'd follow him, he told me I had to go in his car. He didn't answer when I asked how I would get back to the shop!

As soon as we were at the police station, I was put in the slammer! I hadn't the foggiest notion of what was going on, and he nor anyone else could or would tell me what I was doing in a jail cell?

Finally not being able to sleep with all the questions in my head, a cop came walking by my cell about 3:00

a.m. I asked him if he could tell me what I was in jail for
– everyone I asked didn't know. He said, "Non-support
charge"! I told him it was false, and if I could make a
phone call, and he approved. I called my sister, and told
her all that had happened.

The same morning I was ushered into court, a lawyer
was waiting for me, and I reiterated all of the events of
the day before. This is the first time I learned I had been
"arrested", though nobody ever told me, all had evaded
all my questions!

We were all heard in the judge's chambers, and as near
as I recall after these many years, is what transpired, as
near to the words I remember.

Judge to my wife – "Did your husband ever pay you
any money for support?"

My wife – "Yes, he paid me for the last 3 weeks."

Judge – "Well, if he paid you for the last 3 weeks,
why does the charge say, 3 months, if you've only been
separated 3 weeks"?

Wife – Pointing to the clerk of court, "I told him 3
weeks, and he said, 'well, let's make it 3 months"!

My lawyer interjected with; "You have arrested a man
on two false charges, and I contest this action, and ask
for his release."

Judge – "Well, we have to have this heard in open
court."

So we went to the courtroom, and the same questions
were asked, in addition to my own testimony that I had
given her cash, which she admitted to. The odor of booze
came from the judge – he must have been hung over!

Judge – "I find the defendant guilty and sentence him
to 2 years, suspended, with orders to continue payments,
etc., etc., as I and my lawyer were shocked at my being

guilty of nothing but 2 lies – lies as admitted to by my wife and the clerk of courts! Some of the judge's words were missed by me, as my lawyer slammed his fist on the judge's bench, and stated, "I appeal! I haven't heard anything as ridiculous in all my years at the bar"!!

The result was appealed to the Superior Court, which ordered me to pay support, which I always did anyway – I've never shirked my responsibility, and eventually all was dismissed with some unknown Latin phrased definition I've long forgotten.

Meanwhile with the support payments, and still paying board to another sis with whose family I lived, and for 2 years still paying for bills, mortgage, insurance, etc. I just existed on enough money to get to work, and that's about it. And though I had threatened divorce, never had money to pay a lawyer, and when I could my wife wouldn't sign the papers?! Every time she took me to court, the judge would cut my support payments. That would anger my wife and she'd get another lawyer. The third time in court the judge said, "Sell the house and split the money down the middle! I'm tired of seeing these people here"!

You see, from the very beginning I told my wife she could have the house and furniture; I just wanted the equity I paid into it, which only amounted to $525.05. She wanted everything for her selfish being. My lawyer asked me if I would give him half, if he could settle the case, and so I did, for he was not only a good lawyer, but a wonderful person. When the judge rendered his decision, the lawyer took his half, I got exactly $525.05 – and selfishness got nothing – nothing that is, except bills for 3 different lawyers, the last one also billing her for broken eye glasses she busted, when she busted him in the nose, because she lost all around. When I saw her throw the punch, I exited the side door!

The above may be long-winded, but I thought the corrupt actions of the so-called arresting officer, and the lying clerk of court, plus the inebriated judge, is typical of how people can hurt others, whatever their selfish motives may be.

After the above there were periods of no work, and jobs for some reason I was let go, "on orders from the front office", I was told, and every time after my supervisors telling me how satisfied they were with my job performance – even as to getting quick raises for my work.

I injured my back on one job and was laid up for 10 months, and even though my boss and owner of the shop, had to help me up off the floor, when working under a truck – denied I had injured my back in his employ!

On two different occasions I had to turn to political people to get a job as I was in desperate straits. Though I got these jobs from my state representatives, they never asked for anything, except "don't forget to vote for me". One rep also told me of a veterans assistance program where I received a monthly stipend that kept me afloat while injured, which I was grateful for, as I never knew such a program existed. When I was finally employed, I repaid the money. As for the reps, they are there to help constituents, and as there was no corruption involved, and I earned a minimum wage, I was grateful just to be working. So there are those in government who do help – because they care.

After losing many jobs at companies that told me they were very happy to have me working for them, these notices coming from out of the blue, I figured my ex had something to do with these job losses, and so I decided I would head west, and so made the long trip.

I got a good job working for the biggest truck manufacturer in the U.S. As I had not worked steady, and the aforementioned problems, I hadn't submitted my income tax forms for 2 years, but wasn't particularly concerned, as I knew I would have refunds coming for those years.

I went to 3 different Federal offices for help, information and forms for the current year, and 2 prior years. None of them had forms, none were helpful at all, couldn't tell me how to rectify my income tax problems, and left me high and dry, as to what I could do.

I finally got hold of one IRS employee, who without looking at my papers, decided I owed money. A few days later I decided to get someone at IRS to help me, and one man, stating that he was the office manager reiterated the fact I owed money. Trying to find justification as to who the original person was that said I owed money, I was told, they didn't know who he was, but I had to pay this sum anyway. All my attempts to find this man led nowhere and the insistence I "pay what I owed".

After returning home, I realized I needed an answer to a question, called IRS and asked for the office manager, giving the man's name, and was told he wasn't the office manager, he was just a clerk!

In recounting my experiences at the IRS to a fellow employee on my job site, he told me he was a tax preparer and had all the forms I needed, so I had him do my taxes.

As I just made the deadline for filing, I figured all was ok. And as I had been called in to the IRS in my home state for mistakes in figuring my own taxes, both times I received a refund. I was told that they pulled my file, discovered the mistake I made and so I received a bigger refund than expected. So off that information I assumed all IRS offices worked alike. So when I received a refund for my 3 year filing of present and prior years, I assumed all was satisfactory with my returns.

Many months later I was called in for an audit, and the ensuing result told me I was being ripped off by the IRS. I called my United States Senator, a well known figure, and also my local State Representative. Both sent me to high caliber lawyers, presented them with all my forms and paperwork, and both told me I didn't owe any money at all. But both said, "You might as well pay the money, they'll get you anyway". I asked why I should pay money I didn't owe? The response by both lawyers was, "Because you don't have money to fight the IRS so you might as well pay them"!!

I held out for 4 years. In the interim, the company I worked for did not want to pay for Christmas or New Years Holidays, so would lay off low seniority men to "save money". Though I had seniority on a call back, if it were a layoff of a couple of weeks, I would collect unemployment insurance. If it were to be for a month or two, I would get another job to hold me over until the call back. This happened every year.

When the holidays arrived, I was laid off, and knowing I would be back on the job in 3 weeks, I went down to the unemployment office to sign up for unemployment stipend. They told me they had a job for me. I told them I had worked for the company for 6 years, that I was going to stay there, that it happened every year, and at my 56 years, needed their pension and benefits I had been paying into for those 6 years. So that week was ok for unemployment benefit.

The next week I went down to sign up, and was told they had a job for me, and if I didn't go check it out, I'd receive no unemployment benefit. So I checked the job out, figuring I would just state my above reason, and refuse the job.

I told the supervisor in this new job I didn't want the job for the above reasons. He said, "You're hired". I stated a number of other reasons why I didn't want the job, and every time I gave him a reason, he would say repeatedly, "You're hired"! Then the light lit – I was being railroaded into this new job whether I wanted it or not! And I knew as soon as I started work there, my wages would be garnisheed by the IRS! I was mad as hell for a long long while. I'd had my downtimes, but never in my life was I so embarrassed and insulted to have had this happen to me. This company was in cahoots with the Federal Government. Sure enough, starting my second pay check they took half my pay for 2 years, for by this time, the purported money "I owed" had snowballed into 3 times the original false debt, with all the added penalties and interest!

Well, after my "debt" was paid, I had to go to the main IRS office. There I was met by some over weight head honcho and what looked like two IRS agents, who looked like a couple of "Mafia Suits"! I signed papers acknowledging payment. On the way out the head honcho said, "Don't bother to call your Senator or Representatives, it won't do you any good." Guess what my reply was – two words – F and Y!! To finish out the story – I was called back to my original job after I paid my debt. And I sat in the General Managers office and listened to his spiel about what a nice job it was, and all the rest of his propaganda, noticing men working whom I outranked in seniority, who had been working all the time I was on the other job having my wages garnisheed. When he got through extolling the company, I said, "I wouldn't work for you or this company if it were the last job on earth." And I told him very bluntly where he could put his job offer. So both companies work in cahoots with the U.S. Government to screw the little guy around, while the biggies walk off with their corrupt millions. No matter, I still have many friends from that job that I see frequently. At least they know me and what I stand for.

If you think outsourcing and insourcing jobs is a recent phenomenon, you had better think twice. In the job I was forced to take by the government, the company had a policy in place, of hiring immigrants, rather than hire American Citizens. I sent men to my new place of employment because the money was better, so were benefits, etc. These men were never hired. The men hired, whether knowledgeable about the job or not, were immigrants put to work by the Federal, State, County and city governments. All these entities subsidize the company, they don't want the immigrants jobless, or hanging around the streets, or on welfare, so this, and I would surmise, many other companies are forced to hire these people, and many American people are not hired. And they are people with 10-20 years of experience in their trade. This has been going on since my work there in the 1970's and 80's. And like everywhere else, if you have a political connection, you get management jobs and promotions! And as this is a Union shop – there has to be some accommodation between the Union and Government subsidized companies!

There are times in the past when I've had to work 2 and 3 jobs to keep my head above water. A few of these jobs were as night manager of a gasoline station. Part of the job forced on people that work in these stations, is scamming customers into unnecessary auto repairs. I've been told to tell the customer something is badly in need of repair under the hood, worn belts, hoses leaking, or any number of things, just to make an extra few bucks on the people who knew nothing of mechanics, especially most women who probably have never looked under the hood in their life. I've quit jobs like that – when I'm forced to lie to people to keep a job, is when its time to quit!

In coming to this new state, I stopped to fill my tank, and used the restroom. On returning to my car, I was told by the station attendant that if I was driving any distance, I'd never make it, as my rear end was leaking oil, pointing to oil spots on the ground. This idiot didn't know me from Adam, but I knew his scamming tactics. I told him I'd take my chances. I not only made it the next 400 miles, I drove the car for 9 years before trading it in for a newer model. Oil, schmoil!!

While here in my new area, I and other musicians went to an Eagles Club. One or two people wanted to make changes, to have more activities, especially music and jazz sessions, to raise money for the club. One of the instigators of this new approach was made Secretary-

Treasurer. It wasn't' a year before he took off for parts unknown - with the money!

The same exact thing had happened back home, the same way, by the same type of people of good will that want to change things for the better. In this case two of our dearest friends took off for parts unknown – of course they also took the treasury! Both Clubs folded!

I also joined another nationally known club, won some money in a pool, which couldn't be located. In checking, a former employer of the person responsible for my "lost" money, I discovered that another man had won $400 in a football pool. That money was also lost. The same person responsible for my loss, was responsible for that loss, and was fired, as the cash register didn't tally with the number of increased customer patronage. So the donations for children and other civic endeavors from me are gone, and I wait for the demise of that club.

Some years ago I started going to Arizona to look for gold. It was a kid's dream of finding gold, and something I always wanted to do. Through a friend of mine, we went to his uncle's ranch, and were taken to a mining claim he owned, and proceeded to learn placer mining, sluicing and panning gold bearing soil. And it was a boyish thrill when I did find gold, and it was fairly easy to find in that area. I made many trips to visit my new rancher friend, way out in the boondocks and I enjoyed the pristine country, and being far from the big city for weeks, or a month at a time, doing this for about 10 years, so I knew the man very well, and knew of the following episode first hand.

Over the years the city of Phoenix has outgrown itself, as to water resources. It was decided to build a dam to collect water from a few small streams and rivers to fill the dam. It was also planned to pump water from the Colorado River into the dam, to ensure a future supply of water to the City of Phoenix.

In doing so, the ensuing build up of water would back up into countless canyons and ravines, gullies, so much so that people would have to abandon their homes and property. The Bureau of Reclamation began the proceedings of takings by Eminent Domain from my friend and 3 of his neighboring ranchers. That was legal except my friend who had the best piece of acreage of the 4 ranchers, was offered less money than the rest of the ranchers. He made many trips to see the official in charge of the Bureau of Reclamation, and even taped one of the meetings. I have heard this tape – all smoke and mirrors, lies, promises made, but not kept by the Bureau. They wanted to take his land alright, but not on the same terms as the other ranchers received, but much less fair market value than these others. Nothing was agreed upon, and all prior arrangements were abrogated by the Bureau by their unfair practices and lies. My rancher friend was given a certain number of days to abandon the ranch, even while still negotiating a settlement.

One day while visiting my friend for a few weeks, we were returning from Phoenix with supplies for the ranch, and were flagged down on a dirt road by a local sheriff. He told us the Feds were coming out the next morning to move my rancher friend off his property, lock, stock and barrel. He tipped off my friend as they had known each other for years. My rancher friend was angry that the government people would break their agreement, forcing him off his land, while he was yet legally on his property, as the termination date to move was still a week or so away. The surprise raid was to occur the next day.

Early next morning we awoke, my rancher friend strapped on his 38 caliber pistol, and sure enough, here came this convoy of semi-trailers through the fence with a couple of officials, and a lawyer representing my friend. I was indeed a bit scared, and worried to see my mild mannered friend angrier than anybody I had ever seen, pacing around, agitated no end, with the gun on his hip. I knew he was a good shot, being a Marine! Usually if he came upon a diamond back rattlesnake, he would pick it up and throw it far away, for they are a necessary part of nature. But if there was a snake around the ranch house area, he would kill it, as he and his wife had had close calls with snakes around the ranch house, their dog having been bitten a few times. And I had witnessed him one time, on finding a snake sunning himself about 30 feet away, taking the head of the snake with just one shot!

All of us including the truck drivers and helpers, were on pins and needles, as we knew we were going to see a "shootout", just like in the countless western movies we had seen.

It took about 2 or 3 hours of gently talking and cajoling my friend to sit down and work something out. So for the better part of the morning we did that, his lawyer and I softly talking, and working out an agreement getting him to give me his gun. The agreement was a fairer price for his land, plus the government would pay for the moving of every item on his property, paying storage until he found a new place to live. It was a very nerve rattling morning to say the least.

I had admired my friend for his easy demeanor, honesty, and hard worker, his being a Construction

Superintendent, knowledgeable about mining and geology, so that I took to reading books about our Earth. I only saw him twice after that, on his new land, and learned a bit more of his resulting ending of the above situation.

Though he didn't receive the promised amount for his land, he at least received enough to buy another piece of land. The government reneged on paying the promised storage fees for all the construction steel and timber, hardware, barbed wire, numerous valuable pieces of equipment, as he was also in the process of building a new house, which I also was involved in, so much stuff I've forgotten the number of semi-trailers used to haul this stuff away.

This honest, hard working man had been lied to for so many years, and screwed around by a corrupt Government Official, as to come close to killing any number of people, is shameful to have reached that point.

And to continue to break agreements, witnessed by a number of people, including me by a government stooge – who by the way – is now a member of the Arizona State Assembly!!

My friend informed me of another incident involving another Senator, who now serves in the U.S. Senate. It seems this person bought worthless land, way out in the boondocks in the desert. People figured he must be crazy to buy all that land. Years later the State of Arizona built a series of canals for irrigation of the many farms, growing cotton, fruits, and revitalizing cattle ranches. How co-incidental it is, that these canals ran through all the land this Senator owned, making him a millionaire for buying this previously worthless property! I'm not an investigator, I have only seen and experienced many things, and can usually depend on other things told to me by others I consider to be honest and trustworthy – I simply say, you have read this far – go figure!

Thus far you have read of mostly my experiences with corruption, ethics, moral degeneracy, both in low and high places. These experiences are shared by millions in America, not just me. And what is the response from the American Public? Next to nothing, for we have no power as individuals to make necessary changes. Only when a group of people band together in a common cause, can change come about. The little guy, in desperate need is helpless alone, hence the seeking of someone who can help. Sometimes a "connection" helps, but most always is the money. It always takes money to rectify an insurmountable problem. Just to publish this book will take the majority of my limited income. To have the book reviewed and possibly appear in a newspaper or magazine book selection review, will cost 2000 dollars. Marketing the book will cost thousands more. A losing situation for this old guy on limited funds.

To illustrate not only the above, but a very recent occurrence as to the need of money to rectify a terrible situation, not only affecting me but thousands, if not more people in this country.

I have had a number of episodes of tainted food with E-coli from one of the nation's biggest supermarket chains. I have all the medical records, my going so far as to saving the tainted food. Lawyers won't help because I have no money to fight this corporation. And the danger from these imported and home grown diseases aside, think of the cost to doctors, hospitals, medicines, incurred by people who are sick, and die from these infections. And how many people like me are fortunate to have Medicare, supplemental insurance to cover the costs. And who ultimately pays for all of this? The American people, not the guilty corporations. Yet we have no recourse to any of this danger because we have no money or political connection which would also take money, in order for a politician to be galvanized into interceding in our behalf. And if the politicians are on the take from the Corporation lobbyists, we are dead in the water! As I write this, there are countless news stories of recalls of tainted food, poisonous toys, and numerous other items dangerous to the American people. Does our government do anything to help put a stop to this? Absolutely not! There are so many lobbyist payouts to our corrupt officials; they do not want to stop the Quid pro Quo! The above, with all its attendant disastrous results, are what the people endure because of outsourcing, our once proud Big Business Conglomerates foistering sub-standard imports on the American people. When I was young, we called it, "Junk from Japan". Now it is Crap from China!

As this is as nearly chronological as I can remember, I will state two more items of what I consider corruption. In destroying one of the most basic American rights – the right to vote in an election.

As I had 2 neck operations, I thought it best to move back east and live with my sister. While there, the National election for president was held. Being duly registered to vote at the same time as I registered my vehicle, I went to the polling center with my sister to cast my vote. They would not give me a ballot! When I inquired why I wasn't allowed to vote, the Polling center worker told me, "The Attorney General doesn't believe in your party"!! I had never heard of anything more ridiculous in my life. I told the worker that my party was legitimate and duly recognized as such, and the candidates were printed on the ballot. He replied with the same remark, and all my entreaties were in vain. I was angrier than I had been in years, but I realized if I raised a big fuss, I could be arrested for disturbing the peace, and maybe it could have been a Federal offense, as I was involved in a Federal Election fracas. I had no choice but to leave, because some biased official made such a stupid decision, and my insisting on my Constitutional right would land me in jail!

I decided that wasn't a state I wanted to live in, medical condition or not, so I returned to my state I left a year and a half ago.

Then the next election for president, and other voting items was here, and again I went to the polls, being duly registered to do so. About half way through the process, the voting machines malfunctioned. All we voters complained, and all we got were shrugs of the shoulders. We weren't told to come back to vote again, just the shrugs and lots of non-answers. So for the 2nd time in two presidential elections, my votes weren't allowed. I have talked to every Representative and Senator, or their office staff about this flagrant denial of my right to have my vote counted. It's been over 2 years with no response from anyone.

Another situation is of a personal relationship which is ongoing, but shows no process of being resolved to my family's satisfaction.

About a year and a half ago one of my sisters entered one of the nation's top well regarded hospitals for an operation. The same was a success. While there, someone gave her a test and decided she had a beginning symptom of dementia. To this day I don't know who gave her the test, or who made the prognosis. With my experiences of all of the above, I have no doubt that the person making the decision, is connected to a nursing home as that is where my sister was sent, and has been there since.

Being 3000 miles from her, I am of little help. Telephoning my sis twice a week just isn't enough. My niece, who has never had responsibilities, is the only family member who does her best for my sister. Working her own job limits her assisting in anything pertaining to getting my sister released. Also her lack of knowledge and limited income precludes legal assistance.

My numerous phone calls to Government Agencies supposedly in place to aid those suffering civil rights violations, has only resulting in my being shuffled off to some other agencies, eventually ending in a vagueness of explanations, and ending in maintaining the status quo – in other words, they are not interested – the situation remains the same.

I went back, hoping I could alleviate the situation, by getting my sis into an aftercare facility. On limited funds, I bunked with my best friend, the honest cop mentioned previously, as I had no vehicle. He did all he could for me, took me wherever I wished, until I felt I had worn out my welcome, as he naturally had his own priorities and could only give me limited time for my endeavors.

We realized that the connections or honest lawyers we knew, were passed away, or moved to other locations unknown. That one important avenue was no longer available. The only other way was money – and that I don't have. Money solves many problems, other than necessities, as food, shelter and bills!

I visited my sis every day, I constantly asked to talk to the nursing home doctor (many times) I never was allowed to do so, even though on one visit he passed right by me. They evaded all my entreaties, telling me to make a call for an appointment! I have yet to be contacted by any doctor in over a year.

While visiting my sis, I was constantly joined by a nurses aide, who stayed with us, even going to the lunch room, or walking the corridors together, this person was always within earshot. Upon questioning this, I was told my sis had to be monitored 24 hours a day. Even though I'm by her side? What they were afraid of was, I might whisk her out of the nursing home.

My sis lost the apartment of 20 plus years, her furniture is gone with most of her possessions. Much of her personal items have been stolen while in the nursing home – no one can answer how or why or by whom. I have no doubt it was stolen by the insourcing of cheap nurses' aides from Africa, who speak next to no English, and understand less!

If you wonder why the many forms of abuse go on daily in these homes, it is very simple. I can get after care in 2 places where I live, less than 10 minutes from my home, and would cost less than $2000 a month. This nursing home, and most throughout the country charge at least $120,000 a year! Like I said – go figure!

But to be admitted to these nursing homes, a person has to get rid of any savings they may have – in my sis's case, very little – then who pays the bill? Easy to figure – Medicaid – how? Thru your and everybody else's taxes. These homes are corporations – so lets figure – I am a lobbyist – I give you X amount of money, along with your co-workers who are all politicians, and you corrupt government figures come up with some phony way to get all the elderly into these homes, and warehouse them for as long as they exist!! That's a lot of warehousing for anyone 60 to 100 years old and a hell of a lot of greenbacks to the politicians and corporations!

Connections – while in my home state, the buddy I stayed with, we both visited a very nice woman, who reminded me of my own wonderful mother. She gave us homemade pie and ice cream, we had very enjoyable times conversing with her, a very nice lady indeed. One time we took her to a fine restaurant for lunch.

She has the same dementia as my sis. She has no day care, but lives alone until her daughter returns from work. Why the discrepancy you ask? Coincidently- her son is a former State Senator, now working for a big corporation, and so with his influence ensures his mother doesn't' have to endure what my sis and other do in their prisons.

After effecting no success with my sis's incarceration in the nursing home, I received a call from my niece – my sister had fallen and broken her hip. Nobody in the nursing home knew how it happened. In calling the home for information, the answers were always evasive. I asked, if she were monitored 24 hours a day as I had been well informed, why didn't anyone know how she fell and needed a hip operation? "Oh, came the reply, we can't afford to monitor people 24 hours a day, we're shorthanded." Huh! That was in complete contrast to what I and my niece and brother had been told – and the reason I was constantly shadowed by a nurses aide on my visits!

Then she broke her eyeglasses – again they don't know how – monitored right?

There are many things of a nature one could consider minor, but to the nitty gritty it's nothing more than abusing the elderly – as I got your money for the rest of your life – so who cares!

My sis has always been self reliant and active, so seeing her walking the nursing home floors on her own, the nurses would rather see her sitting in a wheel chair, like most of their "customers", comatose, tongues lolling, drooling, and mostly unattended, rather than seeing my sis walking around on her own.   Nursing home care? Care less is the rule!

Trying to get info to help my sister, and seeking the proper way to go, I called all the Senior Organizations I've been donating money to for the past 30 years. I was rebuffed by people telling me, "we don't get involved in that", or, "we can't help you". In repeating my problem, stating I didn't ask them to help me, I only wanted to know how to proceed or where to go. All I got were their "no help" answers. They are as phoney as the rest of Government, and will never get money from me again.

In my neighborhood, less than 200 feet of my home is a meth lab. I have smelled the odor of various substances being cooked countless times. Others in the neighborhood have also detected the same. There has been a steady stream of customers to this lab to buy drugs. Neighbors have called the Sheriff's Department; have given license plate numbers of many vehicles of these buyers. Though the law officers have been to the house and meth lab, the man is still in business. Not only has he been running the meth lab for at least 5 years, he also has at least 2 driving under the influence arrests, an assault arrest, drives a vehicle without license plates – he is still free as a bird and to my knowledge, has never been arrested for any drug violation!

$1 + 1 = 2 = $ Opinion

In the preceding pages you have read of my personal involvement in various events, or personal knowledge of the same through my trust of honest people who also experienced similar happenings.

After a lifetime of a multitude of countless occurrences, I have developed one simple philosophy – 1 and 1 equals two – very simple, and one of the first things we learn at school. That equation will never change. However there are those who will have you believe that 1 and 1 equals any number they choose. These are the corrupt people. These are the people that work primarily in Government positions and in big business "special interests". Or if they are ordinary American citizens, they have been hooked by the bait of propaganda that would have you believe one and one makes 9, or whatever. Then there are the same type of Americans who have more loyalty to the above people, or their corrupt political party, than they do for the U.S. Constitution and the rule of law. 1 plus 1 equals a positive truth.

Based on all of the foregoing, I have developed my own opinions and have many questions, which I advance for your own conclusions.

Last year I attended my annual Air Force Association Reunion of WWII Vets in Washington, D.C. One of the events on our itinerary was a trip to the White House for a meeting with President Bush and a photo op. I told all my buddies I would rather meet Mafia Don, John Gotti!

I have no use for people that intentionally lie, and so the 3 things that decided against the White House visit were, the lies about weapons of mass destruction, the undeclared war in Iraq, and admitting he lied, for when questioned about this by a news reporter, Bush replied, "so what, we got Saddam Hussein didn't we!" Along with the above, you will understand why I have no use for this White House Dictator, or anyone connected with him. Bush stated that God told him to do it! Was this an I pod text message? Who is his God? Satan was a God expelled from Heaven, from what I have read. Is this his God? Did he hack Bush's cyberspace?

Regarding God, and the Law. Who's law do we live under? Our founding Fathers attributed our being to the Creator, Divine providence, supreme judge of the world, and so wrote our Constitution, borrowing from God's Law. God's Law is the Ten Commandments. Our laws are basically the same. But corrupted people everywhere want to remove these commandments from "public" places. Any mention of God is being objected to by these same corrupt people.

If these laws are null and void, then so is our Constitution! I have never heard of a Catholic, Protestant, Jewish, Muslim, or any other faith having exclusive rights to God! There are many names for Him, Allah, Budda, Bacchus, of simply God. Whatever the name he is just that !God! So if God's law is not THE law – every law written under the name of God are null and void. We are living in Anarchy! All laws are null and void! What do you think?

Let's see now – my Mom and Dad, God Bless them – taught we kids the rights and wrongs of life and living, and all things in between – the rules they set down for us. Where did these rules come from if the rule of God's laws are null and void, and our great constitution is also negated, along with every statute we live by in our own cities and towns? Are my parents liars? Did they make up rules of their own? What laws do we live by – or whose?

We see our lying Bush making laws as he goes along, claiming Executive Privilege. Dictators also made their own laws. The Congress aids and abets all these new rules. Osama bin Laden also makes his own rules – he's so sure of his rules are correct – he is hiding in the mountains. Bush hides behind all the mountains of corrupt congress people and special interests!

Looking back at all the wannabe kings, emperors, dictators on the trash heap of history, I side with the rules set down by my Mom and Dad, I'm sticking with them. They understand 1+1=2. They understood the truth, God and our founding fathers. Dictators never show love – but my Mom and Dad did!

Speaking of the above 1+1=2 – did you ever think about the old ploy used by politicians for eons, "don't point fingers"? This is a blatant attempt to make the above equation equal 23 ½ or sum such propandist number. For in truth, if you point a finger you will find out the who of the problem, usually a person, in political life. As a mechanic, if I told you your carburetor was your problem, when I knew it was your alternator, your problem wouldn't be solved. Or an electrician telling you to replace your table lamp, when your electrical outlet was shorting out, or a plumber saying you needed a new faucet, when in fact, your plumbing system was clogged – you wouldn't solve the problem.

So this mindset, this is the way Politicians and Special Interests work. Never point a finger, never fix the problem, just create new problems to cover the old. Governments never solve problems – they create problems! Just look around your community, state, Federal, so what else is new? Usually the finger pointer, the whistleblower, is the one who suffers. Did you ever hear of a whistleblower who was rewarded for his efforts. Read my foregoing episode of my hometown buddy, the Honest Cop!

And how about all our Heroes in sports who take illegal steroids and drugs? Is it any wonder? I've read books written by CIA agents who admit being involved with selling drugs, on an International scale! So why is our government "fighting" a drug war? The CIA are mercenaries who deal drugs, assassinate heads of state, foment revolutions, sell weapons to our enemies, and are involved in all sorts of clandestine activities that are detrimental to our country. They are a secret governmental authority, evidently answerable to no one – just as our so-called people employed by corporations in Iraq and elsewhere, i.e. Blackwater! They are answerable to no law in the world. The American "S.S."!!

The FBI and CIA hate each other – that is why we are never forewarned about impending disaster. They won't share information! Information that would have saved thousands of lives in this country!

They never shared, or informed higher authorities of the Kansas City, Murrad Building information they had. Never shared information on the Twin Towers, or any of the highjackers that killed thousands of innocents, always destroy forensic evidence, hindering any investigation of the Twin Towers, Kansas City, Waco, Texas. In fact, if you look at all the failures, and mis-management of many events that have happened with these 2 agencies, you will find those in charge of screwing up these events, received promotions! Read books and decide!

In reading one book of the events of 9-11, one thing disturbs me greatly. In the case of the plane that supposedly crashed in to the Pentagon, and Flight 93 that crashed in Pennsylvania, one weird item stands out. Both planes were said by Government officials to have "vaporized", as there were no airplane parts, yet there were purported remains of people and luggage! I have also read that according to an expert, the plane would have been flying over 3000 miles an hour – faster than the speed of sound! Now being a WWII Air Force vet, I've seen many crashes, explosions of bombs, ammunition, and gasoline, many times overseas and in training. I've never seen an airplane "vaporize", "liquefy", as was reported. Even if one "liquefied", one would expect melted metal to be seen! I'm afraid that explanation will "vaporize" if the facts become known!

Although we have had dictators in the White House since President Roosevelt, none as bad as this inept wimp we have now, who would like everyone to give their life for "his" country - he opted out of Vietnam and was reported AWOL. An experienced fighter pilot who never went to war? Other people who did multiple tours, and he didn't do one? The only battle he had was with alcohol, and from what I have read – drugs. (The book is in your local library.)

Let's see now – contrary to what the Constitution says about Congress having sole responsibility to declare war – we have President Johnson, and his failed 10 years in Vietnam, oops! – forgot Truman and Korea – plus Nixon and his debacle with Vietnam – everybody's hero with his one-liners, Reagan- and his Iran-Contra war – Clinton and his sellout in Bosnia, and the ongoing farce in Iraq and Afghanistan!

Isn't it strange – we start all these wars, don't know how to fight them, and then blame the people we attack, because they can't solve the problems we started in their countries?

I thank God, that though I volunteered in WWII, I'm glad I didn't stay in, or join the reserves – I might have been long dead! I don't mind serving my country – but I'll be damned if I'll serve some idiotic self-serving politician who is only interested in bullying other countries for power, self aggrandizement, money, for control and world domination. That's why we don't win wars anymore, we don't want to – world control is the reason! And as many have contended, even former head of the Federal Reserve Bank, Alan Greenspan – it's all about oil! You say you don't believe it? Read about all the oil fields and investments by the Bush family spanning the last 3 generations!

Still in doubt about world domination by the U.S.? Read on -!

According to my monthly Air Force magazine – a few months ago there was a hearing in Congress to cut the number of Air Bases we control all over the world. I had long told people we had bases in 130 countries, everyone thought I was nuts!

The Air Force article said the Congress would cut 400 bases from the 6500 bases we have in other countries! Yep! 6500! Now that wouldn't be bad if they were plain old airfields we were using for transnational airlines – but these are military bases, probably paid for by money to some country scrabbling to make a living. There is one big difference. As an Air Force crew chief on a bomber in WWII – that's all I did – I was a mechanic responsible for my airplanes air worthiness. Today all airmen are additionally trained as infantrymen and in the same tactics as infantry! So instead of holding wrenches and so on – these people are taught to fight battles – so now you have a force of men, probably in the hundreds at least, who have the ability to engage in a ground war. 6500 bases, hundreds of men – that's a lot of troops! Multiply those troops, plus 160,000 in Iraq, 20-30,000 in Afghanistan, and only God knows how many more we don't know about, equipment, weapons, ad nauseum – do you think world control is hogwash!!? Every country Russia has vacated, we have taken over! Again read! Perpetual war for perpetual peace! What a dumb assessment!

Let me state here what I believe as the start of the takeover of the U.S. when the UN was formed after WWII, unlike the congress of WWI that refused to join the League of Nations, the now post WWII Congress began its march to corruption unlike anything before. They approved of all the foreign, unelected bureaucrats proposals in the UN rules. Our chief delegate who also promulgated many of the rules was Alger Hiss. This abhorrent excuse for an American Citizen was the top Russian spy, "working for our government"! Even tho all this is known by our politicians and government officials, our idiotic traitorous people who are supposedly representing the American people, always shun our Constitutional Law, and use UN law to go to war – all completely illegal!

It makes no difference who is president; they are all feeding at the same trough of power and money. These people are selling their Mother's and are so blinded by money; they can't see that it is counterfeit! They are so interested in building their "legacy", they can't see they have built a legacy of crap; they are like pigs in a trough, wallowing in mud and garbage!

Case in point – my local congressional rep, who was the chairman of the House Ways and Means Committee, and held the purse strings for certain projects presented by other Congressmen. A bill came up in Congress to ratify the North American Free Trade Agreement. It may be free but it is not fair! As many in Congress were going to vote against the treaty, my Congressman was sent out to "twist arms" to vote for the bill. You know what arm twisting is, as Bush says, "you're either with us or against us". Translated, either vote for this bad bill, or we'll "whack" you. Meaning politically – how corrupt you are, or in other ways to discredit it. After the arm twisting, the bill passed.

A short time later, my Congressman was given over 740 million dollars for road construction in our area! Not only that, we have a leaking dam in our area, and it would take 2 million? Dollars to examine the leak. The Congressman only had to make a phone call, and got the money! I doubt if it went through congressional hearings.

Also locally, developers came to this area with a plan to "improve" the area, through enlarging the airfield, which is only to service small private planes. Of course there also would be new hotels, motels, big business box stores, and oh, yes, takings by eminent domain, of many historical places, private homes, etc., to enhance this area, business wise.

This is a historical, pristine valley, with beautiful mountains, a lake, and streams, wonderful scenery, great caring people, and simple a nice laid back area where people from the hectic big city relocate, to the relaxation and easy lifestyle found here.

So to make a buck, the developers want to change everything. They want big city atmosphere and all its attendant ills to pervade our valley, drugs, crime, and all else this change will bring. Although the locals voted overwhelmingly against this, there are few locals out for the buck, and as of this writing, the idea is stalled. But the corrupters don't give up easily and are still working at their wrong headed plan.

Another plan being foistered on another area close by, is to take all the sludge from five big city sewage systems and dump it on our pristine desert areas. Officials of course will benefit – they always do. They don't care for ordinary people, who are treated like the excrement they dump on our beautiful desert country – all for making a few bucks!

Another and most important type of sludge being dumped on the whole of the U.S. are illegal immigrants.

I can hear all the cries of "racist" coming from the very mouths of these law breakers and their corrupt supporters as I write this. So I say to those idiots – drop dead!

My Dad is the first born of legal immigrants – my Mom's family were also legal – but different nationalities. They came here, went into business, educated themselves and were good legal American citizens.

I remember a time when I was about 4 years old, and my Italian relatives were visiting our home. They were conversing in Italian, especially so when we kids were around – grown up conversation. I pulled on my Dad's pant leg, looked up and asked, "Dad, why don't we speak Italian too?" He looked down at me and said very firmly, "Because you're an American, and you will speak the American language." That was it – period!

I grew up with friends whose families were all immigrants, so mixing with other people is nothing new. And all people were here legally. I have worked with, associated and have many friends of many races. Black people helped me play jazz music, we visit each others homes. Latino's invited me to play with their music groups, and I love that Latino music, Bossa Nova from Brazil, music from all cultures. What you are ethnically doesn't affect me; it's what good that you are in your heart that is important. I have even been invited to play at an important Latino festival, and was the only "Gringo" in the house, playing their music!

Perhaps the best point I can make concerning illegals, took place when I finally found employment in a secure job, when I first came west. I was there only a few weeks when one Mexican fellow worker, whom I hardly knew, asked if I could take him in for awhile, as he had just divorced, had no place to stay, and owed lawyers a lot of money, leaving him near broke. All I had was a pull out couch in my small 4 room house – so he moved in. I never asked him to pay for a thing. While together, I got to know him as a good person, down on his luck. He related to me how he had swam the Rio Grande 9 times to enter this country illegally, and every time he was caught and returned to Mexico. Finally he decided to try the legal way and did so and became a legal immigrant, got a good job in the same shop I mentioned above, and later bought a small apartment complex of 18 units, later sold those to purchase a nice family home for his new wife and child of theirs, born a few years after his rooming with me. All this done as a legal immigrant.

He became one of my best friends, while rooming with me, he asked if I would like to go to Chihuahua, Mexico, to visit his family, so we drove all night to get there, it being Easter weekend. He evidently had told his Mother about me, for the first thing she said to me when my friend Raul introduced me was, "Mi casa, Su casa" – my house is your house! I had a wonderful short weekend in Chihuahua, even visited the widow of Pancho Villa.

So take a lesson from Raul – come here as he did legally, and you can succeed. If you come here illegally breaking our law, proceed to undercut our job market, misappropriate phoney ID's, steal and cheat to stay here, you are not welcome, and you'll never get to stay in my home! And you won't be a friend!

Now there is another kind of person from Latin America whom I've known for years. Though not like my friend Raul, he and I got along well, especially as he knows my taste for Latin music. He told me one time, he belongs to an organization called AZTLAN. This organization is one Mexican group that would like to take back our southwestern states for Mexico. He made the statement to me, "You people stole all these states from Mexico". I replied that there was a signed treaty, and more importantly if we stole the southwest from you, "who did you steal Mexico from?" He had no answer, for indeed, like us, the Spanish stole the country from the Toltec, Aztec, Maya Indians, just as we did with the American Indian. Of course now our President Bush is doing all he can to support illegal immigration, and make Mexico, the United States and Canada, one country!

One other item directly affecting me, and others like me. I am a smoker. There is a 50 cent tax in this state, on every pack of cigarettes. It lessens the hurt somewhat financially, when one knows the money is supposed to be used for educational purposes, chiefly to prevent people from smoking. A recent article in the newspaper told of an investigation into the government entity handling this money, as little, or no money had gone into this program. No one could account for the money, it was just "lost" in the bureaucratic maze of shuffling money around till it disappears – generally into a variety of pockets. I have read of no ongoing investigation as to the whereabouts of these lost millions of dollars! What a ripoff!

The above foregoing pages of incidents however great or seemingly nonimportant, are nevertheless corruptive in one way or another. To illustrate, consider the pretty little snowflake, beautiful in of itself, and even more beautiful in a snowfall, coating the trees, grass and greenery with its whiteness contrasting sharply against the darker colors, truly breathtaking. But take the same beautiful snowflake, scoop them together and you have a snowball, which if hard enough, can maim or kill someone very easily. Also consider what heavy snowfall can do, in causing all types of vehicle accidents, collapsed buildings, from overweight on roofs, avalanches that can wipe out towns, derail trains, disrupt communications, smash houses with falling or blown over trees in blizzards, and many other catastrophes.

So it is with one little act of a favor, one little white lie. Just like the innocent beautiful snowflake, that soon becomes a snowball, all these little things done for the right intention, soon become snowballs of corruption until today we have a virtual blizzard of corruption inundating this wonderful America that has the same result of too much snow. And as always in any catastrophe, the innocent people are the sufferers of this disaster. There is one big difference, one is an act of nature – the other is blatant premeditation designed to hurt or destroy innocent people, and all for money and power.

THE SELLOUT OF WE THE
PEOPLE BY THE UNITED
STATES CONGRESS!

The crooked bribing lobbyists have been around ever since the U.S. Constitution was ratified, and most likely before that. They have spread their dirty money everywhere to influence political figures for the benefit of special interests.

Nowhere has this been more blatant than in the U.S. Congress. Though the corrupting activities are many, only a few are necessary to show how this blatant illegal activity has hurt every citizen of this country in countless ways. Congress should work for the people, they are our hirelings. Contrary to the Constitution, we are their slaves.

Witness the Federal Reserve Bank – strictly unconstitutional. Only Congress has the right to coin money. Yet the Congress abrogated its responsibility, giving it over to the Federal Reserve Bank. The U.S. borrows money from the Federal Reserve, at interest, causing inflation, and through years of this debt, borrowing for wars, and countless other illegal activities, we now have a debt to the world of Ten Trillion dollars, all through the use of this counterfeit money, that isn't worth the paper it is printed on.

When I was young, my Mom sent me to the store to buy groceries. I had a ten dollar bill, on which was a gold seal. On the front of the bill was a notice that the bill was redeemable at any bank for 10 dollars in gold!

Then President Roosevelt, by his own illegal decision, took this country off the gold standard. From then on we have had silver certificates of paper money, only payable in silver. President Nixon then reduced the value of the dollar, so now we have counterfeit Federal Reserve Notes backed by nothing!

All the above is strictly unconstitutional!

Again when I was young, and all this manipulation of money created the Great Depression, there was a Government Propaganda slogan, "Prosperity is just around the corner". The people's rejoinder was, "What corner?"!!

Another ploy to take your hard earned money is the Internal Revenue System – strictly unconstitutional.

This tax was not written into the Constitution, for if it had, there would not have been a need for the 16th Amendment, written by the Congress, to tax our income! So these corrupt clowns take our money and at any whim, give it away to all and countless foreign governments, dictators, pork barrel schemes, ad nauseum, supporting foreign wars, and of course our own illegal wars, and keep us working people broke! There have been people who have fought against this illegal tax, and have won their cases in the courts! How many pockets has this illegal tax filled?

Since WWII, just about all presidents have been involved in illegal wars, or illegal activities in other countries, and undeclared wars. Only the Congress can declare war!

Again the corrupt bribers (read lobbyists) spread their money through the greedy congressional ranks, who then habitually abrogate their responsibilities and vote on some cockamamie UN resolution, which is not even a legitimate government, to go to war. Meanwhile the pockets of the special interest war mongers and our corrupt Congress are filled with the booty from these illegal wars, and again the dumb American citizen pays for his stupidity in allowing this scum to perpetrate these evil wars on us. The money we lose pales in comparison to the precious lives given up by those patriots, and the sacrifices of these heroes and their families. Congress has sold us out on every so-called war for the last 60 years!

Would that I could claim to be a writer – I can't do that in comparison to all the great writers of the past and present. I can claim to be a good musician, and good at my work ethic, as avowed by my employers. I like to think I'm a giving person, especially to children with disabilities, and other kids. I have also had a curious mind, and like to see answers to my queries. To me, and I reiterate, 1 and 1 makes 2, and always will. So I put forth to the reader a broad synopsis of observations based on all of the foregoing, and also put forth questions for the reader, as perhaps other, and more learned people than I can supply the answer to my 1+1.

FICTION OR FACT?

If I wanted to control the world and everyone in it, I would use the following method, in part or as a whole, and perhaps much more methodology to accomplish this.

I would intrude an ersatz government entity into the most powerful country in the world and use its contrived laws to eventually usurp the laws of this host government. I would use the well documented ploy of propaganda slogans to entice the population to my thinking as a beginning program to change the mind-set of the population, such as – "wild and scenic, endangered species, threatened kangaroo rats, birds, global warming, etc, for as Adolph Hitler maintained, "If you keep repeating a lie over and over again the populace will eventually take it as the truth".

I would put in place a mechanism to control news, so that people will hear only what I want them to hear, such as Hollywood people's antics, alcohol and drug use, divorces, play up all the idiotic happenings continually twenty four hours a day, but don't let people know the important news of wars or battles, don't show dead soldiers, or any type of news of a negative nature concerning government or big business. Again this is another propaganda ploy.

Play up and scare people through potential catastrophes, meteors, tsunamis, hurricanes, earthquakes, etc. And if these things do happen, be as inefficient as possible, while showing people I am doing all I can to help them, even though everything I do results in detrimental loss to the people.

Continue to inform people of the ongoing war on drugs, even though I am involved in drug running and encouraging young people to use drugs and alcohol. Promote sex from an early age and negate all parental teaching or control. Stick young children with 5 or 6 drugs early on so they will come down with all sorts of physical and mental deficiencies.

During elections, don't use paper ballots, and if so, invent reasons so they won't be counted. Use machines that can be rigged just as in Las Vegas.

Tax people to the utmost so the working class has just enough to exist, that way I have more of their money to use to control them.

Cut the number of days Congress actually works, let them give themselves more raises, vacations, health and medical benefits, overseas junkets, all at taxpayers expense, so that less work is done in Washington, and more money goes into the pockets of politicians. I would also encourage more taxpayer money be spent on pork barrel projects which will keep the corrupt in office, and keep the taxpayer broke.

I would outsource jobs and insource the same, thus breaking the once dominant world producer of goods to a third world status.

Through the above environmental laws, stop mining, logging, ranching, buy cheap inefficient products from other countries , further reducing abilities to produce in this country. Aligned with the above, closed factories of all kinds will further reduce the world's greatest producer to impunity.

Set up a few international communist leaning organizations, recruiting politicians and big business men, so that these organizations will influence the decisions made in congress, abetted by the bribers.

Make secret agreements, without consulting, or the knowledge of Congress, with adjoining countries, to make this one country, and eliminating this once great and free country, a vassal of me and my world dominating group. Along with this, secretly build a superhighway, run by another country, into the host country, taking land by "eminent domain", and owned by foreign entities, further eroding the host government. Continued funding of politicians can easily make this happen.

Encourage illegal immigration by unskilled workers, further eroding the base earnings of countless industries, lowering the standard of living of the host country. This, along with fraudulent mortgage contracts will force people to live in, or next to poverty. Do not let the host country close it's borders or enforce it's immigration laws, or our invasion will not succeed, and very important in this, is forming organizations, using propaganda, to instill in the majority of these immigrants, that they are really taking back a country that was stolen from them. I would also give money to the leaders of the immigrant countries to encourage their cooperation.

I would also employ my bribers to work at getting the corrupt congress to pass all legislation for NAFTA, CAFTA, The Treaty of the Sea, and all other treaties to further reduce the souvernty of the United States.

I would also have to divide the people, using religion. I'd have to get God out of everyday life, in schools, businesses, law and the courts, as our main business is money and power, and we can't have false Gods getting in our way.

Most of all, we have to continue to have wars! Wars are where we make all of our money! If we continue these wars, we drain the country of its youth, and if we also continue to push and maintain the right of abortion, soon there will be no more youth, and taking control of the country will be assured. We must convince people that though murder is a crime, it's ok to kill babies.

We don't want to win wars anymore, all we want is to get the troops stationed in various places in the world when the day comes for a complete takeover. Truman and the UN stopped the Korean War and MacArthur was sacked. Neither did we try to win in Vietnam, source of all the tin and rubber in East Asia. We kidnapped Manuel Noriega in Panama – our co-drug dealer. Got involved in Central America and its drug dealers. Stopped the 1st Gulf War and left stand our benefactor Saddam Hussein. Bombed and took over in Bosnia with a bunch of corrupt insurgents. Used propaganda and a WMD's as an excuse to grab the oil in Iraq – then killing our ally Hussein. We don't want to win a war there, as control of the oil is the goal.

Control of the oil in the Mideast as we know it doesn't stop there. Since the break-up of the Soviet Union, there have been other oil pipelines bypassing the older pipelines to a new loading point in the gulf. The new line comes from the former Soviet Satellites which are some of the richest untapped sources of oil in the world, many owned by the Bush family! One reason our troops are not coming home soon, if at all.

We will use the might of this host country, purportedly the greatest military machine in the world, to subdue any malcontents, meanwhile training our own mercenaries, such as Blackwater, CIA operatives and the like, to form our own command troops, similar to Hitler's SS for control of the world, including space!

We have to control the energy output by stopping the building of nuclear power plants, which will cause brownouts, blackouts, and great shortage of electricity. Also no refineries will be built, as a shortage of refineries will escalate demands for gasoline, causing price rises, further taking money from the fast growing American peasant class, and increasing the money in our pockets.

Inherent in our making money are false mortgages on homes. We will write the contracts in such a way as to confuse the home buyer, who, in not understanding the contracts, will trust in our word, not realizing the contracts are fraudulent, and eventually in a short period of time, will default on his home loans, thereby losing all his money to our fraudulent mortgages. That way we have his money, his home, which we will sell again, thus profiting twice on one home, and perhaps doing this many times. We will control and own all the new developments all over the country, further breaking the backs and bank savings of the dumb American people.

Through the machinations of our bribers in Washington, D.C., and in the various states, we will lease, sell, or give our highways to foreign entities, to form toll roads, taking more money from the people, also thereby controlling transportation in this country, as we can make our own rules for the use of the roads.

We will take over the schools, and in every way, indoctrinate the children with our socialist philosophy, eliminating the patriotic aspects, and religious teachings, and most of all, eliminating parental control. We will tell the children what we want them to know.

This can be done by administering various drugs for "disease prevention" which will be mandatory. These drugs will be designed to eventually cause other ailments resulting in mental and physical problems which will result in a much less intelligent person, and a person easily controlled by us.

We must appoint our judges, rather than have them elected by the people. That way we lessen parental control, and increase our control over all aspects of the lives of children. Between the injected drugs, and our judges, the children will eventually become adult sheep.

In all our endeavors, however great or small, we must continually use propaganda tools to convince the people of whatever we propose. This tool of propaganda is probably the most important of all in controlling how people think. Adolph Hitler used this tool so efficiently that the people of Germany proclaimed him a God.

Thus far we have convinced the majority of people of our environmental agenda, endangered species, anti-mining, logging, ranching, closing roads and forests, and especially Global warming – all through our constant use of propaganda slogans by our various paid scientists, corporate businesses, politicians we control, and all through our ingenuous use of propaganda. The people are being blindsided from all directions by our propaganda ploy and are becoming like sheep and easily manipulated.

One of our most successful accomplishments has been the loyalty to both political parties by the sheep. The "sheeple" are more loyal to the corrupt politicians than they are patriotic to the Constitution. They are too dumb to know that we control both parties. The Constitution doesn't matter any more. They don't realize they don't have a country "For, by, and of the people". They don't have a country. We own the country and control it and most of the world. The money we have spent on the politicians through our "lobbyists" has been well spent. Our money has made us the masters.

THREE IMPORTANT
HAPPENINGS AND COVER-
UPS

The above title would have the reader want to put the book down and immediately declare me a conspiracy nut. I would hope you will read on, as I am not, as I am of the opinion that I am a person that things happen to on occasion, that I happen to be at a certain place at a certain time, and just happen to witness things, or meet people, by sheer chance, all unlooked for.

There are those who go in search of Celebrities of all kinds, especially "movie stars". I could care less about these people..yet I have met a couple of dozen – just by chance. The only people I sought to meet were musicians from Big Bands, as music is my first love, and I wanted to meet, and talk to those that I idolized. Those are the only people I purposefully did meet.

And by chance I witnesses two very unexpected happenings the world would be shocked to know the truth of, and also read of one other case that really was a coverup, a case I followed because the explanation was flawed. 1+1 did not equal 2.

The first was the case of Flight 800, a flight that left Kennedy Airport bound for Europe. Flight 800 was seen to explode over Long Island Sound. All aboard were killed. The corrupt officials from the National Transportation Safety Board determined the cause to be an electrical wire in the fuel tank shorting out, causing a fire and the resulting explosion and destruction of the airliner as it crashed into the water in a million pieces of debris and baggage.

I have been a mechanic all my life – from a B-25 Bomber crew chief, to heavy duty highway equipment, trucking fleets, marine engines and installations, and one of the best at my trade, according to comments from my employers. I have never, never seen an electrical wire inside ANY fuel tank!! Any engineer, designer, manufacturer who designed such a configuration is building a potential suicidal bomb! I defy anyone to show me such a design flaw anywhere! The National Transportation Safety Board outright lied!!

Then I read a book written by James Sanders, entitled "The Downing of TWA Flight 800". The book is available on Amazon.com.

After reading the book it reaffirmed my own belief that our corrupt government officials lied as they usually do when government itself is always involved in great catastrophes. I will be brief in my rendering information on the books contents.

Government officials either did not interview eyewitnesses who saw all of the above catastrophe, or ignored these same witnesses testimony, in order to feed their own propaganda to the people via the corrupted news media.

Jim Sanders was a San Diego, CA., police officer of many years, retiring from the force to enter the field as a private investigator. He also had misgivings as to the Government's propaganda, so went to ascertain the truth of the tragedy of Flight 800.

Eyewitnesses told him there were a whole slew of ships in the area, that they saw what appeared to be missiles firing from the ocean, up to the sky. After the explosion, the same ships exited the area at top speed! James Sanders learned that these were ships of the U.S. Navy!

Further investigation led Sanders to clandestinely gaining entrance to the place where the pieces of Flight 800 were being assembled by the Government NTSB, allegedly to determine the cause of the crash. Though government people were wary of Sander's investigation, doing all they could to hinder him, he nevertheless gained entrance to the building and the now assembled TWA Flight 800 plane.

He managed to gather residue from the back of seats on the plane, sent the residue to two laboratories for analysis, the labs determining in individual tests that the residue came from an anti-aircraft missile.

The corrupt government indicted Sanders and his wife, though she had no complicity in Sander's investigation. The main charge against them was Treason, and other charges that I don't remember. The verdict was guilty. Amazingly the resulting punishment for being guilty of Treason was being subjected to community service!! I don't remember all of his sentence, but it was a slap on the wrist, in light of the number of charges leveled against him. I was later to read of his suing the government for wrongful prosecution, and winning his case, though I don't know how much money he got, or if collected.

And though we know of the final result of the downing of Flight 800, the also corrupt news media had never reported this, to my knowledge. Like all very important events that happen, our corrupt government keeps them hidden!

Item Two – Space Shuttle Columbia

It was a Saturday morning. I poured myself an eye opening cup of coffee and sat down to watch the news, approximately 8:35 A.M., Pacific time. Though I could hear a voice of an interviewing television announcer talking to people, I couldn't see anyone. Instead the camera was pointed at the sky. The camera was stationary, it never moved. I could tell that because near the bottom of my TV screen I could see a telephone wire, and the sag in it, typical of telephone wires everywhere. The TV announcer was talking about the space shuttle Columbia returning from space, and passing overhead in the Houston, Texas, area, and the very reason he was there interviewing people and talking about the shuttle approaching the Houston area. He was talking to one man, whose name I won't reveal, but which I have on file. The man stated that he had out of town family visiting them to watch the shuttle, and that his wife had awakened all in the household very early, so that they could go outside and watch as the shuttle flew overhead. He said he saw the shuttle and another airplane.

As I watched my TV, I saw the contrail of the shuttle crossing near the top of the screen, approximately 3 inches from the top. It was about 1/3 of the way from the top down, flying from right to left. Almost immediately I saw another contrail approaching the shuttle, "going like a bat out of hell" toward the shuttle, at an angle of 10-15 degrees, flying in the same direction, below and at the angle above. The shuttle got about 2/3 of the way across the top of my TV screen, when the other contrail merged with the shuttle contrail and a tremendous explosion occurred!

Just prior to the explosion, the TV announcer made the remark about Houston losing contact with the shuttle, which is normal and occurs when the shuttle enters the earth's atmosphere. After the shuttle explosion the TV announcer said they still had no contact with the shuttle! And I hollered, "Of course you dummy, it was just shot down"!! We all know of the after effects of that disaster! The Government coming out with another propaganda explanation about a piece of foam coming loose and putting a hole in the shuttle, causing the explosion! Foam?!! What about the numerous times in the past when heavy pieces of tile come off – they have never put holes in the shuttle and they are a helluva lot heavier than foam!! So with all the hoopla about foam and all the ensuing talk, ad nauseum, I was watching the same station the next day, and again couldn't see the announcer, because of all the propaganda photos the government was showing about the shuttle and all else.

But the announcer was still interviewing people, and one man said – "I went outside to watch the shuttle fly overhead, and I saw the shuttle, and a bunch of planes." Strangely I never heard anyone say they saw another contrail!

And to show you how dumb I can be at times – I have a VHS tape recorder sitting on my TV, all connected, just push a button – and I never thought to turn it on for this anticipated routine return of the shuttle! Then I got even dumber. I said to myself, "They'll never show this again – the government will grab the tape, the announcer, all the witnesses, and God knows what will happen to them and the evidence". And man was I dumb! Never expecting the unexpected, they showed the tape 7 TIMES! And never thinking it would be shown again – I remained dumb 7 times! I never turned on the tape recorder!!

Now we all have heard the propaganda about the "foam" causing the shuttle to explode, and everyone is happy and content – except me – I like the truth – I know what I saw – 7 TIMES!!!

So I have a few questions concerning 1+1=2 ONLY.

1. If the shuttle "exploded" over Houston, Texas, why was the government looking for debris from the shuttle in California, Arizona, Texas and New Mexico?

2. Was the missile I saw launched from a ship off the California coast?

3. Was the missile concealed and launched from a truck somewhere in California, Arizona, and New Mexico or Texas desert?

4. When a shuttle, or any other aircraft or experimental craft come in to land, there are at least 2 "chase" planes, to guide and monitor the vehicle as they are approaching the landing strip. Did one of our chase planes accidentally or otherwise fire a missile at the Columbia shuttle?

5. Did you know that though the government is always trying to scare us about North Korea and it's nuclear weapons, I read in my Air Force magazine, 3 or 4 years ago, that a missile was

found in Alaska, with North Korean markings? Why don't they tell the public?

6. Again, about 1 year or so ago, contrails were seen coming into our country, from the Caribbean Sea. 30 groups of fighters were scrambled from NORAD to hunt for these unknown aircraft. Do you know how many fighters are in one group? Do you know these hundreds of U.S. fighters couldn't find the strange contrails? Do you know that commercial airline pilots did see them? Do you know the outcome – I don't?

7. How many other people in Houston or TV land saw what I saw?

8. Why has nobody reported on this – I can't be the only person in the U.S. to have watched CNN news that morning?

9. Why doesn't the news media investigate what they surely must know?

10. If all of the above is true, as I saw, and also read, you can answer the 10th question! Now with all of the foregoing Flight 800, and Columbia Shuttle B-S propaganda aside, I will state my final chance encounter I witnessed – and this one can be proven!

One added statement concerning the shuttle. Since the Columbia disaster, and for over 2 years, whenever and Astronaut returns to earth, they don't return to our country, they return to Russia, and not by shuttle, they parachute in! American astronauts returning to earth via Russia? Because of a piece of foam? This 1+1 doesn't equal 2!

THREE STRIKES AND YOU'RE OUT!

I live in the mountains, near a beautiful lake, and it is a pristine area. Many times I've photographed the area, at all times of the day and night. I enjoy the quietness, often going out on my deck just to enjoy the peace and quiet, so much lack of noise, I can hear vehicles on the other side of the lake though they are 5-6 miles from me.

Some years ago I went out to have a final cigarette before bedtime around 1 A.M., and enjoying the above solitude. Suddenly out of the corner of my eye appeared this immense meteor, catching my full attention. It was easily in our earth's atmosphere, as I could see molten pieces falling from it, and I likened it to the many TV commercials where photos of buckets of molten metal are poured into other containers in the steel mills. This meteor was bigger than the New York World Trade Center disaster on "9-11", and was easily as big as any surrounding mountains. It was so low and looked hotter than a blast furnace. I only saw it for a few seconds, but it was enough to scare me. I thought it was going to smash into the densely populated area to the south, all sorts of disastrous events flashing through my mind.

I ran inside and turned on the TV for the only 24 hour news channel – and nothing. I watched for 2 hours, again nothing. I slept for 3 hours and turned on the TV news – still nothing from where the meteor might have hit.

I watched and read newspapers for weeks without a mention of the meteor. Somewhere around that time period, scientist had begun talking about the Pacific Ocean suddenly warming up for some unknown reason. They called this warming ocean "El Nino".

Although I don't agree with environmentalists, I did for a year or two subscribe to their periodical, mainly because of the beautiful photos in the magazine they put out called Earth – and I can always learn from somebody else's point of view. And about a month later, in a column devoted to nature's catastrophes in the world, earthquakes, tsunamis, volcanic eruptions, etc., in the last line of one paragraph, dealing with the certain months happenings, appeared the sentence – "A meteor was seen over California." That was it. But at least I know I wasn't seeing things.

In the intervening years, there was no news of meteors. But in those years I have watched TV specials, some I saw a few times, always hoping to see news of "my" meteor on the programs about meteors, comets, meteorites, etc., but never is it mentioned.

A year or so later I watched a program about meteors. The program originated at the Jet Propulsion Laboratory in Pasadena, California. The woman narrating the program was as Astrophysicist. Her name and title were on the left bottom of the screen all through the program. So I decided to write her about "my" meteor. I described all I observed in my letter. I got a reply stating that "That person was not employed or known at the Jet Propulsion Lab."

Here we go again – another coverup! Finally after a few years of watching what only must be "scare" documentaries, I pulled out a big map of California, spread it on the floor, got my expensive compass, and aligned due north of the map with my compass, to find out why the denial of the California meteor.

Lo and behold, my meteor wouldn't have hit Southern California, as I didn't realize, until looking at the map, how California coast line swings to the left – looking north to south. The coordinates showed me that the meteor would have landed off the coast of Mexico, or depending on height and speed, off the coast of South America! So to me "El Nino" is no mystery – it's the meteor I saw!!

Again the more you try to know, the less government wants you to know. Evidently all these documentaries are meant to scare and intimidate people, as is the false news we get constantly. There is a reason for everything – 1+1+2 will forever be the truth, and whenever things don't add up – I ask questions – and you had better be able to prove your propaganda!

While sitting here these many months, attempting to put all the foregoing on paper, many more events have transpired to further convince me that my thoughts and feelings concerning corruption in my country are right on the money.

Everything I have stated, except my opinion, are facts and the truth. I defy anyone to disprove them, with factual proof, and not merely stating I am wrong, with nothing they can put forward to disprove my facts. Most of my early experiences were common knowledge and practices everywhere, the status quo, always a part of life, and taken for granted by people everywhere. So people abet corruption one way or another. So if you abet corruption, you are corrupt.

Rather than expound on recent events would only be an exercise in conjecture, not facts. But the events only open my mind to ask more questions, and to apply my formula to these questions regarding 1+1=2.

One important thrust of this book is the fact of the United States Congress, and also our state and local governments, have sold out their souls for the buck. Their treasonous acts over the years have destroyed the American people and the country they have sworn to serve. When these corrupt people take the millions of dollars of campaign funds from the "special interests", they have to pay the money back to these people in the way of "favors". And like the Mafia, if you don't pay back, you are subject to the same punishment the Mafia will inflict on people who double cross them.

Treasonous Congressional Sellouts of the American People and The Plot to Destroy America

1. Income tax – Unconstitutional
2. Federal Reserve Bank – Unconstitutional
3. CIA drug involvement – Our government funds the CIA
4. Illegal Immigration – Congress ignores the law
5. Voting - Congress condones corrupt machines, uncounted votes, Supreme Court not authorized to settle elections, only people.
6. Congress allows - Council of Foreign Relations – Many in government and Congress are members of this Marxist organization.
7. Freedom of the Press – Congress condones Press being controlled, and news censored by owners.
8. Congress - Allows pork barrel schemes for favoritism to pass hidden from people.
9. Congress - Allowed outsourcing and insourcing of jobs, destroying American market, and manufacturing, resulting in job losses.

10. Congress - Allowed Bush to sign secret agreement for Union with Mexico and Canada without Senate overview – Unconstitutional.
11. United Nations – Congress allowed unelected UN to set our environmental laws. Unconstitutional.
12. Congress has aided and abetted over a half dozen Unconstitutional wars, killing and wounding hundred of thousands of our troops and civilians.
13. Congress allowed the abortion killing of babies, but punish others for murder.
14. Congress allows foreign entities to take over our roads and other entities paid for and owned by the American taxpayer.
15. Congress has encouraged bribery in the Congress – a blatant crime.
16. Contrary to our writers of the Constitution, Congress has allowed God to be ousted from our schools, public places and our lives.
17. Congress allows the White House Mafia to make its own rules, secret agreements, and to subvert the Constitution.
18. Congress allowed teaching of sex, homosexuality, lesbianism in school – parents have no say.
19. Congress condones no new nuclear plants or refineries to the detriment of the American people.
20. Congress has more loyalty to a political party than the Constitution.
21. Congress has condoned fraudulent mortgages, causing people to lose homes.

22. Congress condones selling our toll roads, owned by the taxpayers.
23. Congress works less days than the American people, yet have better pensions, medical care, perks not written by the people nor voted on.
24. Congress has abrogated its legislative authority and has allowed a dictatorship in the White House.
25. Congress has condoned the president's signing statement to take precedent over laws already passed.
26. Congress condones the president making decisions as to who can have nuclear weapons – we set the precedent – who are we to decide?
27. Congress allows forensic evidence to be destroyed in all of our disasters, 9-11, Oklahoma City, Waco, Idaho.
28. Congress allows government employees to be jailed for doing their job, while criminals involved go free – Oklahoma City, Border Patrol.
29. Congress ignores Mexican troops in border clashes. – American citizens, wounded and killed.
30. Congress condones rewarding government officials who have been involved in the killing of American citizens. – Waco, Idaho, Oklahoma City
31. Congress condones deficit spending for all illegal government activities.
32. Congress condones the Death tax – unconstitutional.
33. Congress allowed the Panama Canal giveaway by an ex-president to an unelected dictator, paid by the American taxpayer.

34. Congress condones eminent domain takings for and by foreign entities, secretly making corrupt deals for super highway.
35. Congress condones executive privilege practices by the president.
36. Congress condones the classifying of information that should be public.
37. Congress will not uphold the right to bear arms.
38. Congress won't vote term limits, as it would inhibit their ability to get rich from bribery money.
39. Congress should pass a law to elect judges, not appoint for special interests.
40. Congress must stop giving taxpayer money to foreign countries.
41. Congress should give people access to public lands, we own it.
42. Congress should have oversight of information we give to our enemies.
43. Congress should stop financing both sides in a war.
44. Congress should ensure we stay out of Foreign affairs.
45. Congress should ensure all those government officials of any entity be refrained from any position in the public arena that have been ousted from government due to moral, ethical, corrupt practices, as Larry Craig, Gonzales, Ashcroft, Rumsfeld, Rove, Clinton, Gingrich, Cunningham and others.
46. Congress should ensure that all government agencies who are to act in the public's interest, do so, or be terminated.

47. Congress should eliminate any and free benefits for illegal aliens.
48. Any member of Congress who votes for Unconstitutional law should be ejected from Congress for violation of his sworn oath.
49. Any person who has worked as a lobbyist shall be barred from running for any political office anywhere.
50. Any person who takes money or favors from special interests shall be barred from running for political office.
51. Congress should insist on a free press and freedom of information to prevent cover-ups or public news events.
52. Congress should ensure all veterans receive care due them because of injuries received from approving an undeclared war.

MESSAGE TO CONGRESS

Some years ago I sent a taped "Message to Congress" to the head of the U. S. Senate, Trent Lott, and speaker of the House of Representatives, Dennis Hastert, and other politicians, which I state below, an exact copy. I have also sent the tape to others, who were very interested in my dissertation and asked for my permission to use it for their own clubs and organizations, which I agreed to.

I also contacted all my State Representatives, local and county officials, of my votes being denied, which is in the text of this book. Not a single official has ever replied to me in any form, as to the Message to Congress, or my voting rights. This is typical of how the American people are served by these corrupt politicians!

I am not adding anything to the message, as too much has transpired in this country and the world, and would take another book to expound or comment on various happenings. You the reader can evaluate all that has evolved since the original message, and can draw your own conclusion regarding the post message events.

This is an open letter to what I call a gutless Congress, and has been for so many, many years. This is two fold, to chastise and accuse the Congress of shirking it's responsibilities over the years, and also for the latest insult to me, and every Veteran in the country from WWII.

I recently received a letter from the American Battle Monuments Commission, stating that after 52 years they are finally going to build a monument to WWII Veterans – and they want us to pay for it!

Haven't the WWII vets paid enough? Who pays for the other monument sites that took preference over WWII memorial sites, Vietnam, Korea, Women Warriors and nurses? What kind of an egomaniac builds a monument to himself? This is what you ask us to do. Are we supposed to be as Trajan, Hadrian or Nero, who built great monuments to themselves? This is an insult! If the American people, or the government who oversees the construction of such a monument, are unwilling to come up with the money to build such a project, I would say, forget it!! I don't' think any veteran would want a memorial under these conditions. If you have enough money to pass out to the Russians, Mexicans, Vietnamese, Israelis, or anyone else who sticks their hand out, then you ought to be able to come up with the money to say "thank you" to the veteran – "thanks for saving our freedoms, thank you for saving Freedom for the world – and thank you for enabling me to sit in Congress so I can pass all the wrong laws"!

Any war the United States has been involved in since WWII, has been because of the Congress abrogating its responsibilities allowing others to involve the country in foreign conflicts by other means in undeclared wars. Such declarations are vested solely in the Congress! You have shirked your duties. You condone unelected officials making their own rules, which then become "official" law, all blatantly unconstitutional! If you can't do the job we elected you to do for us – then get out! When did the servant become the master? When did it evolve that "we the people, the masters, became the slaves?" The Congress has become a cancer on the Constitution, and I don't mean a barnacle on "Old Ironsides"!!

Wars are now conducted through executive order, or executive privilege. The only executive privilege the president should have is what the American people and the Constitution give him. Like a runaway horse, the president should be reined in by the Congress!

Through international treaties we have allowed other countries to set our environmental agenda, to the detriment of the American people. Congress allows this to happen.

Many years ago I coined one of my favorite phrases – "The U.S. Constitution must have been a woman, for it has been raped by men for 200 years"! I firmly believe that, as the raping of the Constitution continues to this day.

The rights of the American citizen are secondary to the interests in Washington, D.C. We are now second class citizens. Instead of the government being "of, by and for the people", it has become a government of the politicians, for the politicians and special interests! It's about time Congress woke up – get some guts – do what is right for the people and not for themselves. What is essentially right for the people will ultimately be right for the politicians.

People are tired of the, "I am not a crook" assertions. It is time for the Congress to get some moral and ethical values in their lives. We are rapidly becoming a Totalitarian Government. It seems to me I fought a war to defeat that very type of government, who wanted to destroy a free people. Wasn't there a bunch of guys named Hitler, Mussolini, Tojo, Lenin, who learned they can't destroy a free people? How the Congress can sit there and do nothing while a bunch of unelected bureaucrats make all the rules, using their power and greed – is beyond me. You don't care for the American citizen, you don't care for your constituency. Your ineptness has allowed for bad rule making – not good law – and I say, if you have allowed this to happen – then get out! You don't belong there. How soon do we change the American flag to one that looks like the dollar bill?

In 1775 a Revolution began because of an overbearing, uncaring, intolerant government, denying people the right to bear arms. All the freedoms resulting from that conflict were written into our wonderful Constitution. Today our government kills people who have arms in their homes.

Hitler killed people for having anti-Nazi sentiments – can I or other people expect to have our doors smashed in for having anti-government sentiments? This very letter is protected by the Constitution. Will somebody say, "so what"?

I am saddened by the hundreds of shocking deaths of innocent people in our naïve country. The perpetrators of these killings should be held responsible. Instead they are promoted and rewarded! But do you, the Congress, take any responsibility for these events? Haven't you, by your own ineptness allowed others to make their own rules, escalating a small problem, by denying people redress, when they call for help? Haven't you contributed to the tragedies, because you can't or won't do your job? It stands to reason, that any person worth his salt, would be in the private sector making millions of dollars. Why would somebody who thinks he's that bright and knowledgeable, settle for what a Congressman gets for pay? Public service? Who's kidding who? Greed and self aggrandizement are more to the truth!

Con-men – is that short for Congressmen? Congress puts the country in tremendous debt. We the people pay for the debt while you go dancing to the bank. You have never balanced your checkbooks – how can you balance a budget?

The Congress has allowed this country to be sucked in all over the globe, with troops stationed in countless countries, with over 6500 air bases everywhere. Why? The big war was over 62 years ago! Are we now redefining "One World"? Didn't I read that in "Mein Kampf"? Wasn't that also Lenin's idea?

The Congress has given its rights over to others, thus depriving the people of our God given Constitutional rights. Doesn't that make the Congress traitors? Can you be impeached or tried in court? Can you be accused of depriving the people of our rights?

I am involved in programs to help children, and I've done this for years. I've done my best to help others, have worked hard, and have served my country voluntarily, and yet a weed, bird or a rat has more rights than I.

Our Constitution is derived in part from common sense and God's Law – hence the motto, In God We Trust. But it is unconstitutional to pray in school.

Congress has always had agreements between both of its houses. Now they make "deals", which have always borne the distinction of something crooked. One could continue for hours concerning the foregoing and much more, all legitimate reasons for continuing, for this has been going on for a great number of years.

Once this country produced great statesmen, Washington, Madison, Jefferson, Franklin, and many, many more. Now we have the deal makers. The Mafia also makes deals.

I've stood on the bridge at Concord, walked Lexington green, climbed every step in the Bunker Hill Monument, lived on Old Ironsides for one summer when I was young, I've walked the Freedom Trail, walked the Old Granary Burial Grounds, where Adams and Hancock lie, and Freedom is deeply ingrained in me, plus respect for my fellow man and God.

So those who would take away my freedom to write this will prove only one thing – that I am right!

CONCLUSION

You have read of my experiences of corruption of all types. My opinions, formed by my witnessing this corruption, are also noted. There is also my "Message to Congress" which no politician has ever responded to.

I am cognizant of an old adage I heard many years ago – "never believe everything you hear, and only half of what you see".

Remember – if it waddles like a duck, quacks like a duck, looks like a duck, it must be a duck. If someone tells you it is a fox – beware!

Always remember 1+1=2, Always!

P.S. Do you think it's O.K. to say, "GOD BLESS AMERICA?"

END NOTES

Since writing this book two years and more ago, many things of a corruptive nature have occurred in this country. To write of these important events would necessitate another book. To be brief – I randomly took three days of my local newspaper encompassing one week, and marked out all items dealing with corruption in all its forms. Day one had 30 items, day 2 contained 45 item, day 3 reported another 30 items. All items ranged from the least corrupt actions, ticketing of all types of driving infractions, hit and run accidents, drug offences of all types, murders, especially between teenagers, or family members killing other family members, rapes, child molesting, spies in this country, telephone and internet wire tapping, bribing of officials, corporate bonuses of corrupt bank officials, the Madow case, Congressmen who have investments in Health Care companies, Mexican drug cartels bribing our and their officials, the ongoing seizure of marijuana groves by our police in our mountains, run by Mexican citizens, few who are ever found, selling state assets the people own, not the politicians, illegal taking of property by corrupt officials and judges, hundreds of people fired for elder abuse, cheating political officials of their spouses, parents giving kids alcohol, the list goes on and on, at nauseam every day, week, months – forever – these noted about are on a few.

The country that once was the envy of the world, is now the most corrupt of countries anywhere.

As for personal experience noted in this book – there were 4 people indicted locally for killing 3 elders in a local nursing home, by the forced feeding of drugs that caused their deaths. The same thing happened to my Sister in her nursing home after being given the same drugs. No official I contacted before her death, or after, has ever responded to any of my correspondences or warnings I made before hand.

And the repeated ignoring of my written and spoken complaints to all my government representatives in my complaints of the denial of my right to vote in two National elections.

Unconstitutional bank bailouts, the takeover of the Auto industry, now the attempt to have a government healthcare system, are all corrupt measures to enslave the uncomplaining 'sheeple' in the ongoing scheme to enslave the American people.

Dictatorship, tyranny, communism, socialism – call you what you will, we are all victims of our own lack of guts to stop the abuse of power of those who would and do control us. We aid and abet all of the foregoing and are reaping the harvest of a rotten crop of corrupt officials who have raised nothing but failed crops of people.

Once upon a time I was proud of my country, especially in my overseas service in WWII. I met many fine people who came to love the American soldier – the real liberators of enslaved people. We made many friends of these people in foreign lands, we were the best ambassadors the United States has ever had, for we gave all we had to others less fortunate, and those bonds of loving friendship exist even as I write.

Now I am ashamed of my once great country with it's corrupt government officials following the failed dream of Empire, with the same false promises to others, as they pursue the unchanging corrupt practices that have turned an intelligent populace into a flock of sheep, who williningly follow the tinkle of the bell that only leads them to oblivion.

I, as well as we the people, who should be the government, are now standing on our heads, while those who represent our wishes fill us with their rottenness – and we let them!

As I stated in my book title, you who aid and abet the corruption through your failure to do your duty as United States Citizens are truly – "We the Corrupt People"! you prove it everyday, in every way – so drink yourself, and drug yourself in to oblivion for that is where you are headed.

RECOMMENDED BOOKS

1. The Downing of TWA Flight 800 – Jim Sanders
2. Wedge – (the war between the CIA and FBI) – Mark Riebling
3. The Conspirators – Secrets of an Iran-Contra insider – Al Martin – Naval Intell
4. The Controllers – Secret rulers of the world – Edward A. Whitney – Global affairs researcher
5. The New Jerusalem – Zionist power in America – Michael Collins Piper – American Free Press
6. The High Priests of War – Michael Collins Piper – American Free Press
7. Breakdown – America's Intelligence failures & 9-11 – Bill Gertz
8. Jim Tucker's Bilderberg Diary – American Free Press
9. Prelude to Terror – Joseph P Trento – the legacy of America's private intel.
10. Into the Buzzsaw – Kristina Borjesson – The myth of a free press
11. Foundations of Betrayal – Phil Kent – How super rich undermine America
12. The Late Great U.S.A. – Jerome Corsi
13. The CIA in Iran – Don Wilber – CIA deep cover asset in Iran

14. Phantom Flight 93 – Victor Thorn, Lisa Guliana – 9-11 mystery
15. The Judas Goats – Michael Collins Piper – American Free Press
16. A Foreign Policy of Freedom – U.S. Representative Ron Paul – The only truth in Congress